ATTENTION, COOPERATION, PURPOSE

ATTENTION, COOPERATION, PURPOSE
An Approach to Working in Groups Using Insights from Wilfred Bion

*Robert French and
Peter Simpson*

KARNAC

First published in 2015 by
Karnac Books Ltd
118 Finchley Road
London NW3 5HT

British Library Cataloguing in Publication Data

A C.I.P. for this book is available from the British Library

ISBN-13: 978-1-78220-131-1

Typeset by V Publishing Solutions Pvt Ltd., Chennai, India

Printed in Great Britain

www.karnacbooks.com

For
Wendy, David, Clare, Isobel, Simon, and Laura

Helen, David, Charlotte, Tom, Katie,
and Jean

CONTENTS

ACKNOWLEDGEMENTS

We would like to acknowledge the role of the International Society for the Psychoanalytic Study of Organizations (ISPSO), which created the context in which we were able to develop and test many of the ideas in this book. We are grateful to the participants who attended our talks at ISPSO symposia and encouraged us to believe that we might have something worth saying. We would also like to thank David Armstrong, Nadine Tchelebi, Wendy French, and Simon French who gave helpful comments and suggestions on early drafts of various chapters. Finally, we would like to thank the clients, students, colleagues, and random acquaintances who have contributed in one way or another to the contents of this book, not least in the stories and illustrations that we use.

ABOUT THE AUTHORS

Robert French is a writer and organisational consultant and Visiting Research Fellow at Bristol Business School, University of the West of England. He has co-edited *Rethinking Management Education* (with Chris Grey, Sage, 1996), and *Group Relations, Management, and Organization* (with Russ Vince, Oxford University Press, 1999), and edited the papers of David Armstrong (*Organization in the Mind*, Karnac, 2005).

Peter Simpson is Associate Professor in Organisation Studies at Bristol Business School. He co-edited *Worldly Leadership: Alternative Wisdoms for a Complex World* with Sharon Turnbull, Peter Case, Gareth Edwards, and Doris Schedlitzki. He has also published widely in international journals on leadership, change management, organisational complexity, group dynamics, and workplace spirituality.

PREFACE

Every group, however casual, meets to "do" something.

—*Bion*, 1961, p. 143

Most people spend a fair amount of their lives working in groups. For some it is a generally enjoyable experience; for others just an ordeal to be tolerated. However, our emotional responses can mask a more important evaluation. If we come away from a group event thinking only about whether it was enjoyable or not then we have probably missed the point. There is a more significant question: did the group achieve what it set out to do? It is easy enough to say the phrase "working in groups" but actually *doing* it can be quite another matter. It can even be hard to know whether a group really *is* "working". This has been our experience in all types of group, small or large, formal or informal.

At every moment, each one of us can contribute to helping the group work at the "something" it is meeting to do. Too often, however, we do not do so—for reasons that may be conscious or unconscious. For example, the discussion moves away from the agenda and onto other, sometimes trivial, issues: why do I say nothing? Similarly, in one organisation that we know well no meeting ever starts on time. Rather than challenging this habit everyone has merely adjusted their behaviour and turns up late to every meeting. New members soon learn to arrive late or to tolerate waiting for others to arrive. Why is this pattern of behaviour not addressed?

In many such group settings we can find ourselves compelled to compromise our beliefs and to do things we would rather not do; it is as though we have no choice. We stay silent in the face of decisions or behaviours which, when we think about it, we believe are inappropriate or even wrong. There are many reasons why we do not speak up: fear of conflict, apathy, a tendency to compromise, the desire for an easy life, the pressure to collude or conform, or worry about our own competence, and—underpinning all of these—the anxiety that these states of mind tend to evoke. Equally common is to become blind to what is happening: we are so used to the way the group works that we no longer think about it and just assume that this is the way it has to be. Surely, however, it would be better to assume that the group should actually do what it is meeting to do.

Overview

Our purpose in writing this book is to describe an approach that we have found can indeed help individuals and groups to work more effectively on what they meet to do. We draw upon the insights of the English psychoanalyst Wilfred Bion (1897–1979) to guide our understanding of group dynamics. The approach that we describe relies on the use of attention by group members in order to cooperate in pursuit of their common purpose. It can be summarised in two questions: Are we attending to what the group is meeting to do? If not, have we become distracted from the actual purpose and begun to behave as if we are meeting to do something else?

The idea of attending to the group purpose is so simple that it might seem as though there is little else to say on the matter. However, there are two reasons why this is not the case. First, the deceptively simple notion of "meeting to do something" is in fact complex and problematic as a result of its constituent parts: the complexity of defining the "something" that the group will do, its purpose, and the complexity of "meeting". This sets up a broad range of dynamics that stem from the interplay of multiple factors, such as emotion, motivation, individual histories, patterns of behaviour, power relations, and politics.

Second, the idea that I can simply attend to what the group is meeting to do is not simple at all because of our remarkable capacity to deceive ourselves. Our relationship with the truth is complex. To pursue the truth and to make sense of what is happening in a group requires both courage and the insight to see beyond self-deception. For example, if it appears to me that a group is doing the wrong thing, who is to say that I have not just misunderstood the situation or missed something that was said earlier? If I speak up I could look a fool which might have implications for being taken seriously in the future, for friendships, or even for my career. However, others may in fact be thinking the same thing but also staying silent and so the group continues in its error and deception.

Chapter One: We start with an explanation of the state of mind we talk of as *attention*. A key moment in our writing came when we recognised that we were working with two forms of attention: "evenly suspended attention" (Freud, 1912e, p. 111) and focused attention. The exceptional quality Bion brought to his endeavours seems to have come from his ability to work with both forms simultaneously. With a contemplative eye he was able to work with evenly suspended attention, constantly open to the truth of the moment; this he combined with a scientific eye, giving focused attention to what was happening and concentrating on specific elements of individual and group behaviour.

Chapter Two: *Distraction* is the state of mind that can take over when attention is lost and the group purpose forgotten. This usually occurs because strong emotions, especially anxiety, throw the group off track.

Chapter Three: To pursue *truth* is to be "on track". Bion was writing from within a tradition going back at least to Ancient Greece, which firmly gives the search for truth through the contemplative gaze precedence over action or even thinking: "the beginning of it all is contemplation". (Pieper, 1990, p. 72) Because evenly suspended attention remains open to the truth of the moment it can have a transformative impact that leads to the development of new knowledge, although it may feel more like intuition than certainty.

The remaining chapters describe Bion's insights into the aspects of working in groups that require the application of *focused attention*.

Chapter Four: The ability to *cooperate* is fundamental to the experience of working in groups. We draw on Bion's idea of "groupishness" to explore the tensions that arise from the fact that each group member is a unique individual but also a part of the group. This individual–group tension is not only embodied in our external relationships but is also an ever-present tension in our internal worlds between the desire to belong and the desire to be separate.

Chapter Five: We have already alluded to the pivotal role of *purpose*—the "something" a group meets to do. Effective cooperation requires attention to a complex interplay in each group member's experience of purpose. The quality of attention given to purpose will influence each member's ability to maintain a more or less clear sense of their own purpose, and to manage any tensions and conflicts that may exist between that and the common purpose of the group.

Chapter Six: We turn to what is almost certainly the best known aspect of Bion's theory of group dynamics, namely, the three fundamental *forms of interaction* that he observed in groups: dependency, pairing, and fight–flight.

Chapter Seven: One of Bion's most significant contributions was to insist on the unconscious dimension of the dynamics of attention and distraction. *Learning the work of attention* is a complex undertaking and we finish the book with two examples where groups were working specifically on this task. The final example is from a so-called "group relations" event, an approach to learning that was directly influenced by Bion's work.

Insights from Bion

The approach that we describe draws on a range of Bion's writings but the most relevant is the theory of groups that he introduced in his book *Experiences in Groups* (1961). For those who are familiar with Bion's work, it is worth noting from the start that we do not share his focus on dysfunctional group behaviours. Whilst we give great importance to dysfunctional states of mind, our main focus is on the way attention can help groups to work effectively on what they are meeting to do.

Bion's ideas on groups were developed whilst working with colleagues to help soldiers suffering from post-traumatic stress disorder, with so-called "leaderless groups", and then as a psychoanalyst at the Tavistock Institute. Although he had faith in the general robustness of groups, his primary interest was in identifying and describing the factors that undermine effective group functioning. Most of what others have written that draws on *Experiences in Groups* has tended to focus in a similar way on dysfunctional behaviour. We are seeking to redress the balance by giving equal weight to factors that are evident when groups work well.

In focusing on working in groups we have in mind different possible meanings of the word "work". It can mean labour or effort, as in "hard work", but it can also mean functioning OK, as when we say, "It may be a bit old and battered but it still works fine." In work contexts it is all too often assumed that groups function OK through lots of work-as-effort, but it is not as simple as that. Sometimes trying really hard to make a group work can get you nowhere while at other times people can work amazingly well together but seemingly without effort—more like play than work.

The approach we describe here does indeed require a high degree of application—hard work. However, attending to what is important *in the moment*, which is central to the approach, depends on more than just the positive capabilities that express themselves in decisive action. It also requires a state of mind that has been called "negative capability" (Keats in Bion, 1970, p. 125), which depends on the capacity to listen, wait, absorb, reflect, and to remain relaxed yet alert before moving to action (see Chapter One). The fact that a group sometimes works with apparent ease, but at other times puts in huge amounts of effort to no avail, may in part be explained by the presence or absence of a quality of attention rooted in negative capability.

The approach has developed out of our experience of using Bion's ideas in many different capacities—as group members, managers, leaders, teachers, consultants, and researchers. We hope our approach will help make his ideas accessible to readers with a general interest in understanding how to work in groups, as well as to those who are already familiar with Bion's ideas. In this regard it is relevant to mention that throughout the book we use stories from our experience to illustrate the ideas and their implications for practice. All of the stories are true even though some combine elements from more than one event. The identities of all individuals and groups have been disguised.

CHAPTER ONE

Attention

Wilfred Bion had a remarkable capacity for attention—that is, for attending to what *is*, rather than to what used to be or might be, to reality rather than to his or others' aspirations for reality. It enabled him to see things that most of us simply do not notice. This capacity for insight seems to have been based on an ability to give a particular kind of attention, by which he sought to understand his emotional experience in the moment while in the presence of the group—free from hope and expectation, and without memory, desire, or even understanding. (Bion, 1970, p. 43)

Typically, people act as if they *know*. Bion, by contrast, lived according to a much more radical assumption: that what we know is likely to blind us to a far larger territory where, quite simply, we do not know. Attention to this *un*known dimension of experience is at the heart of our approach—that is, to the truth or reality of the present moment and to questions as much as to answers. It is a disciplined way of thinking and being in groups that goes beyond what is required when told to "Pay attention!"

Bion borrows from Freud in describing the pursuit of truth as requiring an approach rooted in "evenly suspended attention". (Freud, 1912e, p. 111) More commonly attention is understood as being "focused", for example on problems, issues, or events. Whilst both forms of attention are important to the work of groups, attention that is "evenly suspended" allows for a greater openness to truth. Milner describes discovering this distinction, finding "that there were two kinds of attention, both necessary, a wide unfocused stare, and a narrow focused penetrating kind, and that the wide kind brought remarkable changes in perception and enrichment of feeling". (Milner, 1987, p. 81) As Williams (2014, p. 35) puts it, "We need to attend, in order to allow what is in front of us to make its impression—not just to scan it for what fits our agenda and interest." Once the "wide kind" of attention has changed how we perceive the truth of a particular moment then focused attention can allow its implications to be explored.

Evenly suspended attention implies an openness that is adequate for engaging with reality in its full sense: it does not focus on anything in particular but pursues truth in completeness. Such truth cannot be known in the sense of being pinned down but it can be disclosed and any disclosure of this kind is transformative for the individual who is exposed to it. Just as a thermometer is predisposed to respond to temperature and a barometer to air pressure, different individuals have a tendency to respond to different aspects of reality. In this sense different individuals tend to pick up, or be transformed by, certain aspects of truth. As a consequence, whilst truth is complete our engagement with it is always only partial.

There are times, however, when strong emotions, such as anxiety or frustration, can cause individuals and whole groups to lose touch with their capacity for either focused or evenly suspended attention. As a result, they can become distracted from their purpose and end up dispersing their energies in ways that are not productive. At such moments, working in groups can involve members in a lot of effort to little effect.

In relation to groups, Bion is best known for theorising this dynamic of distraction. He showed how the complex tensions of group life can cause group members to lose the focus of their attention and to divert their efforts away from their intended purpose onto something else. In the following chapter we will describe in detail this state of mind, which Bion called "basic-assumption mentality" (1961)—an impoverished form of attention that is not directed to the pursuit of truth. A characteristic and perhaps surprising feature of this kind of distracted group mentality, or failed attention, is that group members seldom notice what has happened. If it is pointed out to them that they have allowed themselves to be sidetracked, some or all may recognise that they were indeed feeling uncomfortable and may, as a result, change direction. However, they are just as likely to be convinced that they are working well and already doing what needs to be done.

We have chosen the following story to illustrate something of the relationship between these two states of mind: attention on the one hand, and distraction or misplaced attention on the other. It involves Robert's first ever consultancy assignment when he facilitated a two-day group workshop for the staff of a small business. It shows how he and the group members lost the focus of their attention and allowed themselves to be distracted from the agreed purpose. It turned out to be an object lesson in just how easily such shifts of attention can happen.

> I was consulting to a small co-operative, which was stretched financially. Group members were uncertain about their guiding vision and also experiencing some strain inter-personally. In fact, relationships had deteriorated to such an extent that it had even proven difficult to get everyone together in one room at the same time. However, bringing in an outsider—a "consultant"—was felt by some to be an admission of failure and a betrayal of their co-operative ideal.
>
> It was the first day of the two-day workshop. Right at the start of the morning, before everyone had even arrived, an issue arose in relation to the refreshments. One of the co-op's founding members tasted the coffee and thought it was undrinkable. I felt totally responsible, even though this coffee-loving individual and I had chosen the venue and planned the arrangements in detail. Almost before I knew what had happened I found myself cycling through the town centre searching for a bag of strong, "real" coffee. At 9 a.m. on a Saturday morning I was surprised to find the place almost empty and all the obvious shops still closed.

We will return in a moment to tell the second part of the story but would like to comment first on this turn of events.

This was a moment of real, physical distraction. Robert was literally separated from the group, "pulled" out of the room and into the street. If the pressures or discomfort in a group are strong enough then it is by no means uncommon for group members to shift their focus away from these emotional difficulties. As in this case, they then disperse their energies instead onto some other issue—sort out something to eat or drink, for instance, just get out of the room or push someone else out, anything to escape the uncomfortable moment. For Robert and the group, this manifested as a seemingly innocuous quest for some decent coffee.

What was unusual and somewhat bizarre in this instance was the fact that this literal dispersal happened before the workshop had even begun. On the one hand, Robert felt he was caring for the group in a way that was entirely appropriate; hospitality and mutual care were clear values for co-op members, as well as for him in his role as consultant. At the same time he was unable to care for the group because he was not actually in the room to work with them. He was so quickly put off his stride that it is hard in retrospect to believe he did not notice what was happening; that he had shifted attention from the actual purpose of the workshop—to help co-op members to cooperate more fully—onto providing sustenance for the group.

This series of events points to a key characteristic of such moments: the group dynamic can be hard to spot because you are *in it*. It operates at a deep level, both conscious and unconscious. Paying attention is not always as easy as it sounds. In this case, it seems that in the run-up to the workshop Robert had already experienced a range of emotional tensions that led to his attention being immediately distracted. The strength of the emotions underlying this experience and the reasons for them became clearer as the day progressed.

> During the workshop it became evident that the high anxiety levels that surfaced at the start had their roots in several years of difficult experiences, and may even have been present from the very foundation of the company. In addition, the deep-seated fears of individuals and sub-groups had been boosted by discussions and gossip in the weeks that led up to the event itself. It proved hard to get going before the lunch break and to focus on the task at hand, and the group kept being pulled away from difficult issues and encounters. Jokes and flippant comments were frequent distractions.
>
> However, the tensions gradually eased as the morning progressed especially when certain key individuals saw that their worst fears were not being realised, and that they could talk directly to each other without being blamed or attacked. The emotional issues that had

been festering beneath the surface could be aired and understood. Consequently group members were able to address some important political and practical challenges. In addition, specific action points were developed on the final afternoon and deadlines, roles, responsibilities, and financial implications identified and agreed. As things turned out, the two days went well.

At this time the co-operative was on the brink of collapse but now, twenty-five years on, it is thriving. For us, this experience has proven to be a most powerful piece of learning. It was a very early training in the speed and ease with which attention can shift from one thing to another. In one moment, the focus of attention can be lost and the group's energies dispersed onto something else. However, the situation can also be reversed: if the group's anxieties are well enough contained then awareness of purpose and a sense of task can be re-established. In fact, despite Bion's main focus on distracted states of mind, he retained great confidence in the group's capacity to perform its tasks effectively and in the "vigour and vitality" of group cooperation. (1961, p. 100)

Robert's wild coffee-chase illustrates the way that attention can shift seamlessly and apparently quite naturally from one purpose to another. In this case, the quest for improved cooperation was replaced by the quest for satisfying refreshment. Ironically, one of the problems the group had identified before the event was lateness and now, even before the workshop had begun, Robert's absence made it impossible to start on time. There is little doubt that something was lost as a result but it is also possible that the levels of tension and anxiety in the group at the beginning of the workshop made it necessary for something to be pushed out, as it were. As with a pressure cooker, there may have been a need to let off steam in order to avoid the whole from exploding. For the group even to stay together, they may have needed to put to one side for a moment their fear of the more or less hidden conflicts that might be about to emerge.

This dynamic movement between attention and distraction lies at the heart of Bion's insights: the recognition that when humans come under pressure we tend to respond in one of these two ways. We either stick with it, which requires attention, or we allow ourselves to be distracted from the purpose in order to escape the situation, physically, emotionally, or mentally. Whether we remain attentive or become distracted depends on just what it is that we experience as a threat, on how we experience anxiety, and on our inner capacities and resources as individuals and as a group.

Although it is individuals who maintain or lose attention, these individual responses are influenced and become amplified by the responses of others. As a result, whole groups can appear to demonstrate attention or to lose it. The way any particular group works or does not work can therefore be attributed to the interplay between its members' capacity for attention and their ability to manage the dynamics of distraction.

Bion insisted that these two "states of mind" or "mentalities" exist alongside each other at all times, but he also observed that at any one moment every group tends to be dominated by one or the other. The emotional state of the group is the trigger for movement between the two. Thus, a group dominated by attention will be working more or less well whereas a group that is distracted will tend to make only limited progress in relation to its task because, without anyone realising it, some new purpose has been assumed in place of the real one. In the story above, the new purpose—the quest for coffee—might be taken as a symbol of the quest for the comfort and security of the known. The group avoided the "something" that they were meeting to do because of a fear of conflict and the emotions evoked by the new and unknown.

Working with attention

Attention, then, means sticking with what is—present now, in the moment—however unsettling that may be. If this mentality can be sustained then new patterns of thought and understanding may emerge. Attention depends on *the capacity to stay with the experience of the unknown as well as the known*. In a sense, this formula encapsulates our approach.

The following story illustrates what it can take and what it can feel like to stay in touch with the reality of one's experience. The challenge is to continue to think in the moment when confronted with considerable pressure to be distracted from the purpose, and to retreat from the discomfort of the situation. We see this demonstrated in the way Stephanie did not allow herself to be distracted by the pressure to conform. Instead, she stuck with a question that encapsulated her lack of certainty and, most importantly, she did not give up on what she did not know.

Stephanie was a part of a team that was working under significant time pressures. Her consultancy company's range of services was a little outdated and the management team had made the commitment to redesign the key development programme they ran for senior executives. The design team included four senior client managers, Rupert, Nigel, Miriam, and Stephanie, and was led by the Director of Programmes, Beatrix. Rupert was also working with Beatrix on the design of an innovative programme for the company's most recent new client, an international media company.

Early in one meeting Rupert suggested that the principles underpinning the design of his new programme could form a good starting point for the redesign of the existing senior executive programme. Stephanie thought this was an interesting idea and made a note of it. Miriam said something but Stephanie lost concentration after about 30 seconds, unable to follow the point. She reflected on Miriam's reputation for talking for too long and rambling without any sense of direction. Rupert eventually interrupted, seeming a little irritated, and leaning back in his chair with both hands behind his head. Stephanie noticed his foot was twitching as he outlined the design principles he had developed with Beatrix for the media company. Nigel, who had managed several of the most highly rated senior executive programmes in recent years, responded by reminding the group of some of the successful features of the existing design. The discussion continued in this vein for twenty minutes with contributions from various group members, some adding to earlier suggestions, others treading new paths.

Then Stephanie asked the question that had been forming in her mind: "Do the principles of the media company programme actually match the needs of the market for the senior executive programme?" There was a brief pause before Miriam began another monologue, this time on the changing nature of the market. Eventually an opportunity arose for Stephanie to interject and say she felt it was the specifics that were important—and she repeated her question. Rupert's foot started twitching again. Beatrix explained once more the principles behind the new programme and emphasised how excited the client was about the design so far, and Nigel commented positively about the aspects of the design that he particularly liked. However, no one answered Stephanie's question about the market—whether a generic senior executive programme had the same needs as those of the media company.

Stephanie was made acutely aware of her own sense of calmness in contrast with the continuous twitching of Rupert's foot. She asked her question for a third time, on this occasion adding, "This is a genuine question. At the moment I just do not see it and I need someone to explain it to me." Rupert blustered that it was "obvious" and that "we just need to get on with it". Nigel, however, looked at Stephanie thoughtfully and replied, "I think I see what you mean. I'm not sure we really understand well enough the needs of the potential market for the senior executive programme. Perhaps we need to commission some research."

We see in this story how the pressure to simplify a complex situation can lead to taking an answer from elsewhere and applying it to a new problem. The group was behaving as if the two markets were the same, in effect diverting the focus of attention away from the unknown onto a different and better known object. This dynamic involves an escape into explanation and is a common response to an experience of the unknown—a flight into "knowing" by means of a ready-packaged solution. In Rupert's behaviour, by contrast, and perhaps in Beatrix too, we observe a response based on the frustration of thwarted certainty caused by the inability of others in the group to understand what they see as simply being "obvious". This reaction is also an attempt to escape from the discomfort of the moment; it can be understood as an escape into emotion.

Stephanie's approach, on the other hand, was motivated by the desire for truth. Having become aware of her own uncertainty she is able, after a period of listening, to articulate a clear question, which contains a hypothesis about an aspect of the truth: that there is greater uncertainty within the group than is currently being acknowledged. The hypothesis is uncomfortable for the group because it implies the need for delay, for further thought and debate, and inevitably more expense. Other group members find it hard to respond positively to her question because they just want to get on and do something. This reaction represents a third common way to try to avoid the pressure they are feeling: the escape into action. (On "dispersal" into explanations, emotional reactions, and physical action, see Needleman, 1990, p. 167.)

When a group is compelled to admit "we do not know what to do" it can provoke high levels of anxiety. Stephanie countered the anxiety within herself through disciplined attention to her experience in the present moment. As well as being attentive to the content of what was being said, she also monitored her own feelings of irritation and competitiveness and the feelings and behaviours of others: Rupert's restless foot, Miriam's rambling, Nigel's desire to offer support, and Beatrix's repetition of the benefits of the new programme. Each on its own may have been a reasonable behaviour or intervention but together they formed a pattern that produced a niggle in Stephanie which would not go away. By carefully attending to her inner process she slowly became certain of the importance of her growing sense of uncertainty so that eventually her feelings coalesced into a question.

Stephanie's capacity for evenly suspended attention enabled her to stick with the awkward reality that none of them knew what to do. In this way she took an important step towards a possible answer by formulating a good question, thus giving the group the option of making this question and its implications the object of their more focused attention.

Nigel appeared to understand what Stephanie was getting at and his suggestion of commissioning research into the needs of the market marked a significant shift in direction for the group's work. However, Stephanie did not know in that moment whether this was enough to change the dynamic of the whole group and get her colleagues to appreciate her understanding of their purpose. This was certainly what she hoped when she left the meeting; she even allowed herself to believe it would lead to new thinking from the whole group.

We had no more contact for some months so when we met Stephanie again in another context we were interested to hear how things had turned out. It transpired that shortly after that meeting the company had restructured a range of roles and responsibilities; amongst other things Stephanie had been moved out of this particular group. She told us that the programme review had been scaled back and the market research idea dropped altogether. Instead, Beatrix and Rupert were adapting the format of their new client's programme to match what they thought were the needs of the wider market. In this case, it seems that her intervention as an individual had not been enough to shift the dominant group mentality.

Of course, as we share this illustration we do not know which solution would have been most cost-effective or successful for the purposes of this consultancy group—to follow Rupert's lead or Stephanie's. What we do believe, however, is that as the meeting unfolded it was Stephanie's approach that was most clearly based on attention in the moment.

The two forms of attention

"Attention" and "inattention" are classed in *Roget's Thesaurus* (Kirkpatrick, 1987) as exercises of the mind that underpin the way we form our ideas. The words and phrases listed under "attention" reflect a significant depth and richness to the idea and indicate that the word can be used in both active and passive senses:

> give attention, pay attention, devote/give one's attention to, think worthy of attention, be attentive; draw/attract/hold/engage/ focus the attention, strike one's attention, arouse notice, interest/ excite/invite/claim/demand attention, make one see, bring to one's notice/attention, call attention to, point out, point to.

The word also has certain overtones that help to bring out the contrast with distraction. It can suggest "standing alongside" as an "attendant" does; that is, cultivating a certain detachment from results or outcomes and putting one's own ego or needs to one side for a moment in order to meet the needs of another or of the situation: "A well-developed capacity for attention allows us to be present to what is other than our-selves … without trying to turn that other into ourselves." (Paulsell, 2005, p. 136) Bion's approach suggests a further level to this idea: that a certain quality of attention allows us to be present not only to what is other *than* but also other *in* ourselves. It allows us to become aware of aspects of our inner experience in the moment that have their origins in the group or the wider situation. The capacity for attention makes it possible to perceive these connections, making it less likely that we will simply assume that the other is to blame for our feelings.

The image behind the idea of attending also carries a sense of "waiting"—French, *attendre*—rather than just reacting. To wait can cre-ate a space in which new thoughts or insights may arise, a pause dur-ing which habitual ways of responding may be suspended. This is an emotional and intellectual stance that is often not easy or comfortable, which may, for example, require me to "bite my tongue". Although waiting can involve difficulty and sometimes extreme discomfort, faith in its potential also makes it possible to hold open a hopeful space in which something new may emerge. In his book, *The Stature of Waiting*, Vanstone vividly captures these conflicting aspects of the experience: "an agonizing tension between hope and dread, stretched and almost torn apart between two dramatically different anticipations". (1982, p. 83)

The idea that attention can open a space in our minds is reflected in its etymology. "Attention" is derived from the Latin verb *tendere*, to stretch or extend, implying two positions or forces pulling against each other. Many aspects of the natural world, from the tides to the upright stature of a tree, only function as a result of tension. In animals, the tendons—also derived from *tendere*—help to translate muscle power into movement. Over time, as so often happens with language, this image from the physical world began to take on more abstract or mental and emotional associations. In Latin, the literal sense of stretch came commonly to be used together with the word for mind, *animum*, in the phrase *attendere animum*, that is, to stretch the mind or apply it to something. Eventually, *attendere* on its own came to mean pay attention or listen to, implying an enlargement of one's inner capacities, a stretching and broadening of the mind, which can then be applied to the object of attention. (Barnhart, 1988)

The words and phrases in *Roget's Thesaurus* can be read as reflecting the two forms of attention we have described as evenly suspended and focused. The former is more receptive and suggests an initial process of "taking in", while the latter is more active and implies a secondary process of "working on" whatever has been received. In *Roget*, however, the descriptors of these contrasting modes of attention are merged but they can be distinguished by creating two separate lists.

First, evenly suspended attention—the ability to observe and take in all manner of sense impressions—is reflected in *Roget* in the following terms and phrases:

> take notice of, listen, sit up and take notice, take seriously, miss nothing, watch, be all eyes, be all ears, look into, hear, keep in view, not lose sight of, read, notice, mind, care, take trouble/pains, put oneself out for, be mindful, have time for, not forget.

Second, focused attention—the capacity to process what has made its impression on us and been taken in—is reflected in *Roget* in the following:

> give one's mind to, think, keep one's eye on the ball, focus one's mind on, concentrate on, review, revise, study closely, reread, digest, keep track of, note, recognise, spot, keep/bear/have in mind, think of, take care of, have an eye on, take into consideration/account, consider, reconsider, weigh, judge, comment upon, remark on, talk about, mention, recall, deign to notice, acknowledge.

There are many contexts in which a central role is given to methods for developing the capacity for attention, although they rarely distinguish between these two movements in the dynamic of attention. For example, the first movement in the development of knowledge is the scientist's capacity "to hold in contemplation the self-regulation at work in nature", (Stephenson, 1995, p. 8) which can in turn form the basis of the second movement, the minute and focused observation of natural phenomena. The Kalahari bushman's intense observation of and identification with his prey precedes the focused activity of the hunt. The trained attention of open meditation found in all spiritual traditions— "mindfulness, bare attention, a capacity to be in the moment" (Emanuel, 2001, p. 1082)—can be the basis of a disciplined religious practice. The state of mind Freud described as evenly suspended attention, "an open mind, free from any presuppositions", (1912e, p. 114) precedes and is the source of the detailed and rigorous formulation of hypotheses concerning the patient's condition.

All too often, however, the distinction between these two forms of attention becomes blurred or lost as a result of the tendency to move too quickly, even immediately, to focused attention. Distraction or "failed attention" can arise when focused attention is not based on the observation of truth. Evenly suspended attention is therefore fundamental for sustaining the pursuit of truth and awareness of the group purpose. Without this, the scientist develops knowledge that works against nature as much as with it; the hunter fails to acknowledge the delicate balance between all living creatures and respect for *all* life is forfeited, not merely the prey's; disciplined religious practices become an iron cage of rules that imprison and restrict rather than giving life and freedom, and the analyst merely avoids having to do any more thinking in the diagnosis of the patient's condition.

This state of evenly suspended attention—*gleichschwebende Aufmerksamkeit*—which has been described as "the analytic attitude", also translates as "evenly distributed", "hovering", "circling", "free-floating", or "poised" attention. (Snell, 2013, p. 39) Bion talked of this mental capacity in the analyst as "reverie", describing it as "paying attention to what is happening here and now" and involving respect for truth, for oneself, and for others. (Bion, 1994, p. 139) However, he was not thinking only of the psychoanalytic attitude; he believed that attention of this kind is also "of value in many tasks besides analysis" even stating that it is "essential to mental efficiency, no matter what the task". (Ibid., p. 216)

Attention, then, is a mentality that is central to the group remaining purposeful and reality-based. Its presence can help a group to do what it is there to do, to stick to its overall intention or task, even when under pressure, and to deal with internal and external difficulties and differences without being thrown off track. It is "reality-based" because it does not hide from the truth, however uncomfortable, including the truth of what is not known.

Evenly suspended attention is rooted in the desire to seek the truth and expresses itself in a range of mental dispositions that have been variously described as: patience, observing, waiting, listening, reverie, watchfulness, discernment, and the capacity to stay in the moment without memory or desire. These states of mind have one feature in common: they depend on the capacity to contain emotion without being unnerved by it. This capacity is captured in the phrase "negative capability", which Bion borrowed from the poet John Keats, who described it as a state in which a person is "capable of being in uncertainties, Mysteries, doubts, without any irritable reaching after fact & reason." (Keats, 1970, p. 43)

Negative capability is only negative in the sense that it implies holding back from making a judgement or taking action, if only for a moment. Cornish suggests that this is achieved by suspending "the active intellect which seeks to categorize and therefore limit what it finds", thereby making it possible to refrain from forming "a premature understanding and interpretation of what we experience". (Cornish, 2011, pp. 142–143) Bion argues that underlying a lack of quality of attention in groups is "the failure to observe and [this] is intensified by the inability to appreciate the significance of observation". (Bion, 1970, p. 125) Negative capability underpins the capacity to observe in this way. To work effectively in groups therefore requires the capabilities to practice both forms of attention: first, negative capability which underpins the capacity for open, free-floating attention or contemplation; second, the positive capabilities that allow one to sustain focused attention.

It is worth quoting at length from Freud's description of psychoanalytic technique because he describes so clearly how the capacity to notice is the precondition for the ability to go on thinking afresh:

> The technique ... consists simply in not directing one's notice to anything in particular and in maintaining the same "evenly-suspended attention" (as I have called it) in the face of all that one hears. In this way ... we avoid a danger which is inseparable from the exercise of deliberate attention. For as soon as anyone deliberately concentrates his attention to a certain degree, he begins to select from the material before him; one point will be fixed in his mind with particular clearness and some other will be correspondingly disregarded, and in making this selection he will be following his expectations or inclinations. This, however, is precisely what must not be done. In making the selection, if he follows his expectations he is in danger of never finding anything but what he already knows; and if he follows his inclinations he will certainly falsify what he may perceive. It must not be forgotten that the things one hears are for the most part things whose meaning is only recognized later on. (1912e, pp. 111–112)

These words reinforce the idea that there are different levels to our intention and experience. At one level, we can bring a very focused and minute attention to detail, and at another the kind of broad, unfocused attention described by Freud and Bion. Simone Weil described the former as "a kind of muscular effort", as in the instruction: "Now you must pay attention". However, she viewed the broad and specifically human faculty of contemplative attention as having a far deeper importance. She described it in terms that are reminiscent of the analytic attitude: "Attention consists of suspending our thought, leaving it detached, empty and ready to be penetrated by the object", adding, in an evocative phrase with strong echoes of Bion's writing, "it means holding our minds within reach of this thought". (Weil, 1951, p. 58) In perhaps her most extreme formulation we are challenged to consider that, "Absolutely unmixed attention is prayer". (1986, p. 212)

Attention therefore implies a depth of awareness and level of engagement beyond just focused concentration. It means accepting the need to work with both conscious and unconscious phenomena and with the tension between the longer-term purpose and the experience of the here-and-now. As a result, its impact can be wider than discovering a solution to immediate problems; it can also be seen in terms of development, learning, movement, openness to change, and moments of refreshment in knowing.

Care and attention

When attention is practised in pursuit of the truth and in both its forms—evenly suspended and focused—it demonstrates a quality of care that is unusual and can lead to surprising outcomes. The everyday phrase "care and attention" captures an important dimension of attention in a group context as it raises questions about motivation: What are we attending to and why? What do we care about or for? Bion's concern was to attend to and care about the truth or reality of this group at this moment with the implication that attending in this way can make a difference.

In a group setting the texture of care can often be seen in the attention given to detail—where the devil is said to be. However, according to tradition, the devil cannot influence humans without our collaboration; his talent is to exploit any gap where a detail has been missed. Because it seeks to ensure that the complex reality of this situation at this moment in time is kept in mind, evenly suspended attention is the precursor to focused and detailed attention. The work is thorough, short-cuts are not taken, and previous experience is not necessarily assumed to be a reliable basis for understanding the needs of the current situation.

Sometimes we find ourselves in a group situation which, given the choice, we would rather not be in. However, there are occasions when it is necessary: institutionally and individually we are committed to a course of action and we need to see it through. Such occasions can arise, for example, in groups that have to manage situations where there is a high likelihood of failure, disappointment, or trauma—parts of the health care system, for example, such as a hospice or an accident and emergency department, or those parts of the judicial system that deal directly with the trial and sentencing of offenders. At times, of course, all organisations and communities will have to deal with very difficult situations and they will need groups to meet and take responsibility for doing the right thing. A high quality of attention in such circumstances can be extremely helpful in ensuring that a difficult situation is not made worse by the carelessness that can arise from a climate of distraction. Indeed, it is possible to bring a certain beauty to a difficult experience that is handled with genuine care and attention.

The following illustration tells the story of a challenging situation of this kind in an educational context.

> Appointed as Independent Chair at a forthcoming PhD viva voce examination, Martin was preparing for what promised to be extremely challenging for all involved. It seemed likely that this would be the first occasion in his experience where the candidate would be given an outright fail—despite having had a year to rework her dissertation after a difficult first viva. Martin did his usual preparations but with an added level of care and attention. He made sure that he understood with absolute clarity his role and responsibilities, and the relevant regulations in relation to a failed second viva (never having had to use them before). The week before the viva he visited the room that had been booked making sure that it was appropriate (seating, noise levels, etc.).
>
> On the day of the viva, he arrived fifteen minutes early and noticed that drinking water had been provided by catering services, organised by the research office. At first sight this did indeed seem like care—glasses and water for all. Then, however, he realised that there were only five glasses for six people. (The director of studies, who sits in as an observer and support to the candidate, is not infrequently overlooked.) He also noticed that there was only one bottle of water. Aware that the examination as a whole might last for several hours (in the event, it was four hours long), he arranged for an extra glass and more water to be delivered.
>
> The event was indeed just as difficult as he had anticipated but also went about as well as the situation allowed. After the viva had finished and the candidate had left the room, the examiners would normally take a maximum of thirty minutes to reach their final decision. In this case they deliberated for an hour and a half. Typically

the Independent Chair's role requires him or her to keep quiet, only answering specific questions or clarifying procedural issues that seem not to be understood. However, after an hour the examiners were going around in circles, seeming to know what they must decide but unable to finally commit. Martin used his knowledge of the regulations to ask pertinent questions. They answered each one clearly and decisively. After several questions Martin informed them that in his judgement there were no other avenues for them to pursue. He suggested that this meant that under the regulations they were judging the thesis to have failed. They agreed. With difficulty they made the decision.

When it is good news, the honour of telling the candidate the result typically falls to the senior External Examiner. Bad news is delivered by the Independent Chair. Martin checked that the examiners understood the process. He prepared himself by rehearsing the particular words that he would use. He was aware that by taking up the authority of his role with care and clarity he could make this easier for all parties. Martin tidied the room and before calling the candidate and the director of studies to return he made sure that there were two seats side by side for them to sit in. In the event, the candidate was gracious in her response to the result. It was clear that she was still hoping against hope that the result might have gone in her favour but she understood why it had not. Martin looked at the examiners—all male, all with tears in their eyes. This was hard for everyone. After the candidate had left, the examiners thanked him with real sincerity.

The anxiety provoked by emotionally difficult situations like this can sometimes provoke attention that is focused but misdirected. Without evenly suspended attention Martin might have missed important aspects of this situation and fixated, perhaps, on his own feelings and the challenging aspects of his role. By attending to the details of the meeting and demonstrating care for the process and for all those involved, Martin was able to establish a containing environment for the difficult emotions evoked by the failure of a student. We see the tension in the situation particularly manifest in the examiners, who clearly did not want to do what their roles required them to do. This tension between their individual desires and the group purpose was eventually overcome by attending to reality—by pursuing truth in the moment.

Care and attention therefore require work from the start, which may imply giving attention to detail long before a group actually meets. Typically, such preparation can include not only clarifying broad, contextual issues, such as the purpose, roles, and tasks but also more down-to-earth matters, such as the physical conditions of the setting. In the example below, a manager described to us her first experience of a group relations workshop as a result of which she came to understand in an entirely new way the importance of giving care and attention to detail and the impact of doing so. (See Chapter Seven for an extended discussion of this approach to experiential learning influenced by Bion.)

> The first session of this eight-day group relations workshop began at 2.30 p.m. There were around forty of us and we continued to chat as we filed down the narrow staircase from the coffee room. When we sat down, the workshop director who was sitting with the seven other staff members facing us, the participants, said something like, "At 2.30 I set a time boundary but as there was only one participant here I decided to wait before beginning." Now I guess it was true that we had all left the coffee room at around 2.30, thus making it impossible to arrive on the dot of 2.30, but it cannot have been more than a couple of minutes after. Compared to the rest of my working life we were on time and I felt as if I had been metaphorically slapped on the wrist!
>
> This opening seemed to me to be slightly aggressive and definitely controlling. It just did not seem necessary. This initial impression was reinforced in my mind by the way the staff behaved generally. I found them distant, uncaring, and even manipulative, so that it was hard to trust them. However, on the fifth day there was another event in the room in which we had first met. It started on time as every other event had done up till then except for that opening session. The only difference was that one member of staff had to pop out to fetch a chair because the room was one chair short.

One chair missing. In the normal run of group life, mistakes of this kind are so common that it is unlikely anyone would even have noticed it, let alone read any significance into it. However, this experienced manager described the moment as a total revelation. She suddenly realised that for five days, with around six different events each day, each of which required a different number of chairs and always laid out in a different configuration in every one of the eight or so rooms that were being used, this was the first time that the staff had not put out exactly the right number of chairs in preparation for a session.

Scales, she said, that had grown over her eyes for more than forty years of life in groups and organisations, instantly fell away. She realised with a shock that, far from being controlled and manipulated as she had thought, this was the first time she had experienced a group of managers who were trying with as much integrity as possible actually to do what they had said they would do. On this occasion they had got it wrong because one chair was missing but their slip-up only served to make her recognise that for the rest of the time they had stuck to what they said—to the letter. If we say we are beginning at 2.30 p.m. then that's what we mean and what we will do; what you, the participants, do is your responsibility. And what applied to the details of timing and chairs applied to everything else. The staff members' attention to detail was not a nit-picking over unimportant details, as she would have thought before, but rather an expression of care for the enterprise as they understood it; that is, care for the kind of learning the whole conference was designed to bring into view. She began to see that this was a complex undertaking and required considerable effort on the part of the staff team. Working effectively with this level of complexity requires a high quality of both evenly suspended and focused attention.

To take one example of this learning, it was the first time that this manager—and many other participants, as it turned out—had had the opportunity to examine the impact of lateness and absence and the hidden motivations that can lie behind them. She realised that the observation of timeliness was not merely a rule to be obeyed but was an opportunity to observe habitual patterns of unthinking behaviour. Until then, she had always described lateness and absence as "just one of those things". Now she realised that her projections onto the conference staff as being devious and manipulative belonged rather to the rest of her life—including her own behaviour and assumptions as a manager. From feeling taken for granted and controlled, she now felt cared for. However, she also had to re-evaluate what exactly she meant by "care" because it certainly had not felt like care in the everyday sense of the word. She realised that it was the expression of genuine care for the task or purpose of the conference. The staff's attention to the complexity and detail of the learning process represented care for everyone—but in relation to the overall purpose, not in terms of trying to protect them from pain or discomfort. As the missing chair showed, this did not mean they always "got it right", but attention was certainly the dominant approach of the staff group.

Her final comment to us was enlightening:

> I saw in a kind of flash that they meant what they said. They had made it clear from the start what they were there to do and had done it as best they could—even if on this occasion they had "failed" by counting the chairs wrong. I had come along with a completely different mind-set. I wanted to learn but in reality I somehow expected them to be responsible for what I learned. Now I saw that all they could do was to "offer an opportunity", as the brochure put it so clearly. It was up to me to take that opportunity.
>
> Those two moments—"trivial" lateness and "just" one chair short on one occasion—completely changed how I viewed my whole role as a manager and team leader.

CHAPTER TWO

Distraction

In Chapter One, we began to describe the way in which attention can be used as an approach to working in groups. However, attention is as vulnerable as any other state of mind to the vagaries of human interaction and emotion. The stories we chose were intended to illustrate two things: first, the nature of attention, and second, the way in which individuals and groups can, at any moment, lose the focus of their attention and allow themselves to be distracted by other things. We now turn to this phenomenon of distraction—when attention becomes misdirected, divided, or lost.

One of Bion's key contributions to understanding group dynamics was to describe how and why group members can become distracted and lose touch with the group purpose. It is as if real thinking stops—that is, thinking which relates to the reality of the group's purpose and relationships, internal and external—and is replaced by a kind of sham or as-if, even anti-, thinking. Although it may still look and feel like thinking, actually it misses the point. Instead of drawing group members back to what they are there to do, it draws them away, thereby serving to protect them from the tensions and emotional pressures that inevitably arise when working in groups.

The phenomenon of distraction was so evident to Bion in the group experiences he described—and yet equally clearly not acknowledged by those he was working with—that it became his main focus of interest. It is important, however, to be aware of the context. In one way or another all of these groups were generally therapeutic in aim, involved in studying their own dynamics and relationships; they were learning about and from individual and group experience. It is therefore no surprise, either in relation to this experience or to his growing commitment to psychoanalysis, that Bion's predominant interest was in the cycles of defence, avoidance, and repression. Hence his emphasis throughout on the pain and discomfort that he saw as provoked by "the emotional quality in myself and in the group that is inherent in membership of the group". (1961, p. 116) What he observed led him to an extreme view: that the individual "has to defend himself against his fear of the group—which is known to be indifferent to his fate as an *individual*". (1994, p. 30)

In the "Pre-View" to *Experiences in Groups*, Bion elaborates some of the qualities that can lead to "smoothly running co-operative activity". (1961, p. 11) He describes such cooperation as the expression of a "good group spirit", although adding that this is "as hard to define as the concept of good health in an individual". (Ibid., p. 25) From then on, however, he tends not to describe these qualities in any detail, referring to them instead as if they are rather obvious and already well known. At one point, for instance, he states without elaboration that "[m]any techniques are in daily use for the investigation of work-group function", (ibid., p. 154) that is "smoothly running co-operative activity". His rather throw-away tone here only serves to reinforce the fact that his overriding focus had shifted to distraction—its origins and characteristics, its impact on individuals and their intentions, on the group purpose. His real interest moved from the qualities that support effective working in groups to the phenomena that disrupt it. Others have followed him in saying that both impulses co-exist in groups but have also tended to follow him in exploring only one side.

To describe this defensive state of mind, Bion coined the phrase "basic-assumption mentality" in contrast to "work-group mentality", (ibid., p. 173) rather in the way we distinguish distraction and attention. When in the grip of distraction, the group as a whole behaves as if a new purpose has been assumed and that everyone had bought into an agreed way of operating—their "basic assumption". However, what in effect occurs is that the group becomes driven by their anxieties, their fear of failure or of each other, and so on. The result is that individuals unconsciously collude in the desire to avoid thinking about what is going on, settling instead for an easier state: behaving *as if* they were indeed still engaging with the task while in reality they are doing other things.

When a group becomes dominated by this as-if state of mind, group members shift their attention onto the newly assumed purpose and so lose focus on what they are actually meeting to do. The unconscious aim is to try to make things easier for themselves and to create a situation that is less demanding emotionally and mentally. In effect, the group members unconsciously agree, "we don't want to know because it all seems so hard—and nor do we want to learn or to change." In a group that is distracted in this way, Bion suggested that "assumptions pass unchallenged as statements of fact ... it seems clear that critical judgment is almost entirely absent". (Ibid., p. 39) It can therefore be hard or even impossible for an individual who *does* want to get back to the real purpose to make their voice heard because group members can be highly critical in their judgements of anyone who tries to make them engage with what they do not want to know.

In the story recounted in Chapter One, Stephanie experienced exactly this sense of being unheard or ignored until she managed, on the third attempt, to get Nigel to hear the critically informed question she was asking. To put it bluntly, this group seemed to have lost touch with what it was there to do. The members were behaving as if their purpose was to adapt an existing senior executive programme with minimum effort rather than to transform the programme into a competitive flagship programme for the organisation. Stephanie believed she was attending closely to the purpose of the meeting but it was clear, both at the time and subsequently, that others in the group had other purposes in mind.

When a group is distracted

We have chosen the following story because it illustrates what can happen when a group allows itself to be distracted: focus goes, energy is dispersed into dealing with irrelevant issues, and group members behave as if they had agreed to drop the real purpose and do something else instead. In these circumstances, returning to the practice of attention can be extremely difficult. The distracted group by definition resists giving attention to the real purpose or to the here-and-now reality of the group dynamic. Moreover, misdirected or divided attention of this kind can become habitual, as it seems to have done in this case, where the avoidance of difficulty had become the group's way of operating.

Trevor was a member of a group that had worked together for some years and their current task was to plan an event for the end of the following month. This was the only agenda item. The group was no different to others he had experienced in that the usual emotional, political, and inter-personal tensions—and, therefore, "hidden agendas"—existed alongside the explicit, official agenda.

However positively he tried to approach meetings of this group, Trevor always found that he quickly became irritated by them. The group never seemed to be able to agree anything—or if they did, then decisions made at one meeting were often questioned at the next, or forgotten, ignored, put off, or changed by "someone", though no one could ever say when, why, or by whom. Some things did still get decided and done but many did not and items for discussion were often put off to the next meeting—despite frequently having already been carried over from the previous one. The most striking thing was the way key issues were often swamped by the trivia of group administration in a pattern of delay and avoidance that had became so established that it could no longer be seen. Although his frustration was shared by others they all somehow allowed the situation to continue unchallenged.

In the second of the five scheduled planning meetings, as the normal pattern quickly became established, Trevor tried to manage his frustration by noting down what actually happened. The first thing was that the meeting started late. No change there! Most people were in fact on time but they just sat talking to each other or checked phone messages. It was only after about ten minutes that someone "interrupted" and said, "Oh, X told me she'd be late. Sorry." Then someone else mentioned that Y's child was ill and off school so he had sent his apologies.

On this particular occasion the issue of the missing members turned into a discussion of who had been there/not there the last time the group had met—and then who would/would not be there next time. This led to checking the whole programme of planning meetings because there seemed yet again to be confusion over dates, times, and venues. An additional complication was that out of an expressed desire for democracy the group had agreed early on to share responsibility for chairing meetings and for minute-taking so these arrangements were also checked out and the dates and roles confirmed. Everyone had had so much experience in the past of the problems associated with getting diaries together that they agreed to do it while everyone was there. It seemed to make complete sense to do all this now—quicker and more efficient.

At this point, Trevor wrote: "We've just spent ten minutes discussing the fact that we're not all here! And now another ten minutes sorting stuff we agreed three months ago!" With the ten minute delay in starting, the group had already lost thirty minutes of a ninety-minute meeting. However, Trevor remembers clearly deciding not to say anything about all this for fear of just being labelled a stirrer or troublemaker.

It was only halfway through the fourth of the five meetings set aside to plan this event that something apparently miraculous happened: the group suddenly started working well, drawing on their experience to create a clear vision for the event and to make all the necessary detailed preparations. The "miracle" seems to have been brought about by an awareness of the approaching deadline. Suddenly there was no time to be wasted and their anxiety about doing the planning yielded to anxiety about the deadline.

From the way this group behaved a detached observer might have been hard pressed to work out what its actual purpose was. It really was an "as-if" group—as if they were not there to plan an event at all but rather their task was to get themselves organised. No one asked why it had taken them so long to get down to business nor whether they might learn anything from the experience; it was simply put down to time pressure. As someone observed, "Deadlines focus the mind wonderfully".

A strange part of the experience was that at one level, and despite frustrations, group meetings always seemed to be active and energetic with lots of discussion. In fact, group members often actually *felt* as if things were going rather well: working out dates, times, roles, terms of reference, and so on. However, if anyone had taken a moment to step back, as Trevor did on this occasion, it would have been obvious that event-planning—the group's actual purpose—simply was not happening. They would probably all have *said* that their purpose was to organise the event but their actual behaviour suggested a different reality: that almost anything seemed more important than what the group was meeting to do and so needed to be done first.

The purpose kept proving to be elusive in meeting after meeting. Even though no one had explicitly agreed to a change in direction, it would shift to getting the group organised or sorting out tensions over membership, leadership, or friendship. The alternative activities they engaged in at different times seemed endless: fetching coffee, answering texts, working out dates, choosing a leader, dealing with a problem with another group, sorting out a way of working, agreeing the agenda or a name for the group, finding a suitable room to work in, exchanging email addresses, or just "getting to know each other better". The group members were distracted by all the things they thought needed to be done before they could actually get started.

The problem was that the whole group had become so comprehensively caught up in this dynamic that it was very hard for any one individual to take the necessary step back. The group could only function by *not* attending to what was really going on. They collectively ignored the fate of the group purpose and the way in which they were interacting. Indeed, if someone had spotted what was happening and pointed it out it is likely that *they* would have been seen as the one who was out of step: paradoxically, a call to attention would have seemed like a distraction. It was fear of being judged in this way that stopped Trevor from saying anything about what his note-taking had shown him— especially as he often found himself being the one to question things. In fact, he felt he had become locked into the role of group cynic because others in the group saw him as always making negative comments.

In the fourth meeting, however, things did change. Unlike the situation in Stephanie's story, attention was ultimately established despite the group's habitual attachment to their distractions: the looming deadline seems to have been all that was needed for the group to re-focus in this way.

This movement back on to the task illustrates the fact that attention and distraction are present in every group at all times, however clearly one or the other may dominate at any particular moment. This is why the experience of working in groups always involves a mix of the two. Even though the group can veer off course at one moment, they can return to their purpose the next—and then, often as not, will lose direction again or even find an unexpected, new direction that may lead to a renewal or redefinition of the original purpose. So there is nothing particularly surprising or unusual about this example, except perhaps to note the somewhat extreme way they all seem to have colluded unquestioningly in allowing distraction to dominate their interactions. The story illustrates a phenomenon that belongs to the group and the pattern of dynamics that have become established: it does not reflect a peculiar weakness of the individuals involved.

The important consequence of their extended period of distraction is that they had little time to give to the work of evenly suspended attention. The time pressures forced them to give focused attention to their purpose. As a consequence, it is likely that the quality of their thinking was limited and impoverished and their planning solutions for the event would almost certainly have been based on approaches that had been used in the past.

When group members turn their backs on reality for protracted periods of time in this way they can become incapable of realising their potential, even immobilised. They are stuck with old answers or explanations and trapped in an emotional rut so that they are condemned to re-enact established patterns of thinking, feeling, and behaving that are past their sell-by date. Instead of addressing their uncertainties and facing up to unsettling questions that may imply a need to change, they search for the reassuring, if somehow unsatisfying, comfort and security of the known. As a consequence, energies that might have been used to address the specific tasks in hand are scattered into emotions, explanations, and actions that serve the as-if purpose. An encounter with the unknown may be exactly what is needed but the experience is avoided by behaving as if they already *know*. The unconscious motivation that fuels distraction is defensive: attention is misdirected or divided in order to reduce or avoid any emotional learning—that is, the possibility of learning from, not about, one's emotional experience.

In our private lives this dynamic of distraction can be rather obvious in familiar patterns of behaviour that we choose in preference to what we should be doing. In a similar way, hyperactivity can be a sign of distraction rather than attention: "distraction or keeping busy as a defence". (Emanuel, 2001, p. 1078) It may involve making a drink, clearing one's room, or playing a game on the computer *before* writing an email—or working on email *before* doing an online search—or doing an online search *before* making an important phone call—or making a phone call *before* clearing one's room—and so on; always one thing to defend against the anxiety of something else: "I will not be able to think clearly while my desk [the kitchen/my inbox/the garage …] is in such a state." In reality, of course, "before" in each of these cases tends to mean instead of.

Henri Nouwen (1981, pp. 21–22) has described this state as a kind of disorder of our age:

> Just look for a moment at our daily routine. … There is seldom a period in which we do not know what to do, and we move through life in such a distracted way that we do not even take the time and rest to wonder if any of the things we think, say, or do are *worth* thinking, saying, or doing.

Behaviours of this kind may be more or less amenable to change while leaving hidden the unconscious patterns underlying such distractions. Avoidance of pain in the moment can be the most important thing—emotional, mental, psychic pain—whether it is called "pain" or something similar: discomfort, anxiety, irritation, being "out of my comfort zone", and so on. It may be hard to recognise or accept this as the underlying motivation for the behaviour of group members. In this state, thinking tends to remain superficial and knowing so that, although group members may manage to stay relatively pain-free, they also remain relatively ineffective. In Bion's words, "Mental activity becomes stabilized on a level that is platitudinous, dogmatic, and painless. Development is arrested and the resultant stagnation is widespread." (1961, p. 128)

If, by contrast, the group mentality is dominated by attention to the pursuit of truth then the potential for development is increased. This can include attention to the experience of pain if group members understand that emotions are not necessarily a "disturbance" but can instead be a source of "intelligence" in the sense of useful information. As Armstrong argues, (2005, p. 93) "It is in this sense, it seems to me, that emotion in organizations—including all the strategies of defence, denial, projection, and withdrawal—yield intelligence." A group in this state can demonstrate a capacity to learn from their difficulties without being distracted from their purpose. By recognising difficult emotional experiences as a form of communication, group members can learn from them.

A note on the loss of attention

As with attention, the vocabulary of distraction holds clues to the nature of this state of mind. The word is derived from the Latin *distractionem*, "a pulling apart or separating". A distraction may be stimulated by some external event but it is the internal response that makes the difference, as when we allow ourselves to be "pulled away" by a phone call or a knock at the door. This readiness to be pulled away is reflected in another term Bion used for this state of mind, "evasion" (1961, p. 175)—a "walking away from" or "escape". In the consultancy project we described in the previous chapter, Robert literally "walked away from" the group anxiety when he left the room in search of coffee.

In *Roget's Thesaurus*, distraction appears under the entry for "inattention". However, it does not necessarily involve inattention as we normally think of it—just as a more or less passive state. Instead, Bion observed that when a group stops attending to its purpose, it actively, if unconsciously, shifts attention to something else—as noted in his comment: "At this point the conversation seems to me to indicate that the group has changed its purpose. ... [in order] to settle on [a] new course." (Ibid., p. 31) In this way, the group's attention is misdirected and group members turn their attention to something else. Their energies are dispersed or scattered so that real issues cannot be thought about; indeed, the unconscious purpose is to avoid the emotional pain they believe they would experience if they did face up to those real issues. They can only succeed in doing this if they are able to keep their attention away from the realities of their work together.

Verbs listed under "inattention" by *Roget* include:

> be inattentive, not attend, pay no attention, pay no heed, not listen, hear nothing, see nothing, close one's eyes, turn a blind eye, stop one's ears, be blind, be deaf, not register, not notice, not get the message, not use one's eyes, not click, not concentrate, not hear the penny drop, overlook, forget, let one's thoughts/mind wander, be distracted, be inactive, stray, be put off, be put off one's stride, disregard, ignore, neglect, have no time for, divert one's attention, escape notice/attention, slip one's memory.

A similar sense is reflected in the dozens of adjectives in the entry such as: distracted, preoccupied, engrossed, otherwise engaged, with divided attention, diverted.

A significant aspect of these entries is that, in addition to "no" and "not", there is a prevalence of negative prefixes, which parallel the *in-* of inattention itself; for example, un-, de-, dis-, di-, neg-, a-, non-. The suffix, -lessness, and other phrases such as absence of …, lack of …, also indicate that at the root of these experiences is a sense that something is missing.

This pervading sense of absence or negation suggests something noteworthy about the relationship between the two states of mind that we are considering in these first two chapters. Attention is a mental capacity or capability that reflects the root meaning of both these words: "able to hold much" (Latin, *capax*). We can develop our capacity for attention because the more it is exercised, the more it can expand to include new areas of awareness. However, when attention is misdirected or divided, the distraction always leads to a lack of some kind, a limitation or diminution of capacity and potential: it is a restricted state of mind.

When attention is lost or misplaced it implies denying, avoiding, or resisting the truth or reality of a situation and turning instead to something else—hence Bion's idea of an "as-if" state of mind. Distraction is an anti-purpose, anti-thought mentality, which works to the extent that it allows group members to hide behind something else. However, this is achieved in a thoughtless way and only by "turning a blind eye" (Steiner, 1985, p. 161) to the realities of the situation. Group members can then act as if this other purpose—assumed, not explicitly discussed and agreed—must be dealt with first or instead while the intended purpose is put on hold. The fundamental drive is to escape from, rather than face up to, the discomfort of the moment through superficiality and the reinforcement of the familiar.

Working with both attention and distraction

In our experience, Bion's insights into these dynamics can be extremely practical provided we remember that both states of mind always co-exist at any moment. As a consequence, the relationship between them can act as a touchstone for understanding what is going on in the group. A group that is thinking critically and developmentally gives attention to the reality of what group members are facing and to what is happening to the group purpose, to relationships between group members, and to the group's relationship to its context. Distraction, by contrast, describes a group in which members have allowed themselves to be deflected away from the real purpose and onto a replacement or as-if purpose that may be evident in an excessive focus on internal and external relationships.

Once group members allow themselves to become distracted, they may create an endless range of seemingly purposeful activities. These activities will all have one thing in common: they will be based simply on the desire to avoid the difficulties they are experiencing—both those arising from the demands of working on their shared tasks and those that stem from the challenges of working together in the group. The group wants to do anything but deal with these because then group members would have to face up to the challenges of the actual situation: they would have to face the tough realities, the truth, of the present moment.

Bion described the push-and-pull in and out of distraction as being caused by what he called "emotional drives of obscure origin" (1961, p. 188) that always threaten to divert the group from its purpose—a "development push" and a "regressive pull" that are "built in to the human organism". (Armstrong, 2005, p. 145) This can make staying on track extremely demanding, both emotionally and practically, because attention can be difficult to sustain when the situation is experienced as too challenging—or when it is not challenging enough. Any area of the work may cause difficulties: the broad purpose or specific tasks, the group dynamic, politics, individual–group tensions and interpersonal relationships, the sense of individual and group competence, time deadlines, or some combination of these. In the face of such pressures and the anxieties they arouse it can be a relief to stop thinking for a moment and to put one's energies into something else, forgetting the purpose and the here-and-now reality of the situation. To allow oneself to be distracted means sidestepping such difficulties and thinking about doing something that seems easier—even if this involves stepping away from what one is really there to do.

This is just what seems to have happened to the group in which Trevor was a member. It had, as it were, translated its anxieties about the work into a belief that something needed doing *before* getting started. Thinking in this particular way did indeed help the group to avoid some of the difficult emotions they were experiencing. However, this avoidance did not solve anything. In the first place, Trevor—and almost certainly others too—still found the experience extremely irritating, and second, the actual work did not get done.

Bion had an extraordinary ability to notice when group members became distracted. His most explicit and concise naming of the dynamic comes half-way through *Experiences in Groups* (1961, p. 101): "It is at this point that I say the group behaves 'as if' it were acting on a basic assumption." His phrase "basic assumption" implies the idea of assumption at two levels of significance. First, assume can mean to take on or adopt, as in "they assumed the role of parents for the two children". Second, it can mean take for granted or take as true, as in "I assumed he really meant what he said". The as-if mentality of distraction involves both meanings. At one level, the group simply adopts—"assumes"—the changed purpose. At another level, the new course is also taken for granted—"assumed by the group to be true"— and so remains unchallenged; it is simply treated as if it were indeed the original, real purpose.

The powerful hold that distraction can have over group functioning stems from the fact that it is a *group* assumption. Its impact on group thinking and behaving at any moment depends on the tendency of individuals to become caught up in it and to lose the capacity for independent thought. As humans we seem to be hard-wired for collective action, one might say for tribal as well as for individual responses, so that without conscious effort the power of the group can become mobilised whether for the benefit of the individual or the group. We explore this idea further in Chapter Four in relation to Bion's notion of "groupishness".

The situation is quite different when attention is dominant in a group. In this case, the purpose is only assumed in the sense of taken on or adopted; it is never taken for granted, because attention has a reflexive quality: it can also attend to itself. This is echoed in many of the terms noted by *Roget*, such as: review, revise, digest, be mindful, not forget, not lose sight of, notice, take into consideration, talk about, acknowledge. It not only includes attention to purpose, therefore, but also to the state of the group and its dynamics, to its context and changing external circumstances, and to the relationship between these two elements. Evenly suspended attention means that individuals and the group as a collective remain open to the disclosure of any truth of the present moment that might be of relevance to them and to their activities. Attention may then be focused in any specific area that appears to require consideration.

As a result, attention does not mean group members will simply stick rigidly to *the* purpose whatever happens; instead, they may be able to recognise moments when the original purpose has lost its relevance in some way and needs to be rethought. As Bertolt Brecht put it, "Saying A does not necessarily mean you have to say B. You can also recognise that A was wrong in the first place." (Brecht, 1966, p. 49 [translated for this edition]) When a group dominated by attention changes its purpose in this way, it is not because they *cannot* face truth in the moment but because they *can*. At such moments, however, any new purpose is likely to be negotiated and agreed because it is based on a realistic understanding of the situation in the moment not on an assumed, taken-for-granted truth.

One practical issue, therefore, for any group to attend to is what happens to its purpose. Attention to the purpose—caring about and keeping tabs on what the group does with it—can be an immediately effective way of reading what is going on in the moment.

If distraction or the misdirection of attention is an as-if mentality, then attention might be called an as-is mentality because it is grounded in the search for truth in the moment. As a result, the choices group members make are more likely to be attentive to both the reality of the group's purpose and the truth of their situation moment by moment. If the level of attention is good enough then the group as a whole will be able to spot any tendency to slip into distraction, and individuals will be allowed to remind the group what they are actually there to do.

Both attention and distraction therefore involve a level of group agreement. It is only in a group dominated by attention that this agreement is reality-based: group members constantly put energy into seeing things as they are and to the pursuit of truth, however awkward it may turn out to be. Crucially, a group of this kind does not suppress difference or avoid the new—new ideas or new members—but is able to welcome them.

By contrast, attention can be misdirected and / or divided in response to fear of difference and the new. In this distracted state, individuals can feel they have lost their individuality and their ability to think or act independently and become merged with the group, or like a puppet controlled by the rest. In a group dominated by attention, on the other hand, questions and differing views are not merely tolerated but actively sought, and the collective relies on its members to keep their individual perspectives on things and to speak their minds. Only in this way can they go on thinking, challenging apparently accepted ideas, and acting in accordance with the purpose.

Moving the goalposts

We finish this chapter with a story that shows how easy it is to be distracted from even a clearly agreed purpose. Through the movements within the group between attention and distraction, the purpose can be clear at one moment, then lost, and then found again—an experience which may be replicated throughout the life of every group. There is nothing special or unusual about the story in terms of its setting or content. However, we hope that it does show how what we have learned from Bion influences our thinking in the moment in a group setting, and hence our ability to act.

This story describes one moment during a difficult, two-day negotiation Robert attended between two men involved in a business partnership that had irrevocably broken down.

> The case was heading for court because the two parties had been unable—or unwilling—to agree an amicable financial settlement. Their relationship as business partners, and also as long-standing friends, had gone badly wrong and was now beyond repair. They had only agreed to mediation in a last-ditch attempt to negotiate a solution themselves rather than handing over to the court to make a ruling for them.
>
> Although I had known and been close to both men and their families for many years, I now found myself sitting in one room with just one partner and his legal team. The other partner and his team were in a separate room, while the negotiations took place between their legal representatives in a third space. Despite being with just one of the partners, my brief was clear. I was not to take sides but to support the purpose that had been agreed by both parties: to find an equitable way out of their collapsed business partnership that would not cause the venture to fail. They both cared too much about the business and what they had achieved to allow that to happen. Although they had been fighting for well over a year they were not there to see one side proved right and so to destroy the other. The crucial issue was how to

secure the on-going future of the fledgling business they had created together, which one of them was now taking on alone. The business still needed a lot of nurturing if it was to thrive and take off. This was the purpose I was there to support.

In the event, keeping this purpose in mind turned out to be crucial to the outcome. It made it possible both to steer a path through the micro-detail of the financial and practical issues and to manage the considerable tensions that had developed between these former friends, neither of whom now trusted the other. Each party seemed to believe that they had right on their side and that the other was set on destroying them. As a result, the first response to any proposal from the other side tended automatically to be met with suspicion.

To everyone's relief, I think, the initial negotiations went surprisingly smoothly. Both sides seemed prepared to make constructive proposals and to seek agreement for the sake of the purpose. Then, towards the end of the first day, there came a particular moment when I suddenly realised that for some reason the pressure had become too much and the group I was with had shifted from attention to distraction.

Both sides had more or less agreed which assets should stay in the business and what compensation should be paid. So far, so good. However, just as the negotiator from our room was about to go next door to seek agreement on one final detail, a new issue was raised. Although it did not materially affect the overall sum for compensation, it did affect the timing of payments. The other partner had been refusing to contribute in any way towards the running costs of the business for the previous six months, so someone suggested that an element of the compensation equivalent to the missing six months could be paid immediately as a kind of back payment rather than spreading it out over the next two years. The overall total would remain the same.

It was obvious to me from the general demeanour of those in the room that something else was going on at this point. If I had to put the texture of this new, as-if purpose into words, I'd say it was to teach the other partner a lesson, to get one over on him.

Despite all of the considerable pressures, difficulties, and provocations they had faced, I had admired the way in which everyone had managed to keep their attention on the task in hand. Now, however, the changed purpose was instantly assumed without challenge or discussion. What alerted me to the sudden shift in the group's mentality was the way that the thought of this punitive back-payment seemed to create a certain frisson of excitement in the room.

However, it seemed that I was the only one who sensed that the agreed purpose had unconsciously turned from negotiation to revenge. I questioned the proposal and warned the group that I was pretty sure it would be experienced as a provocation rather than a genuine negotiating position. However, my point of view could not be heard.

The negotiator took the proposal next door but returned shortly afterwards saying that I had been right: the other partner had "gone ballistic" at the suggestion. The proposal was, therefore, simply dropped and the previous arrangement left in place instead. The group returned easily to the actual purpose and a final agreement was put into place the next day without recourse to a court hearing.

Describing the events in this way may make it sound as though this moment of distraction could have been avoided if the group had been able to behave properly. However, Bion did not believe it is ever possible for a group to sustain attention at all times. His purpose in writing *Experiences in Groups* was to argue this point and to explore the resulting dynamics. He argued that because a group is always pervaded by the pressures that lead to distraction, any attempt to establish attention that ignores the reality of distraction is almost bound to fail at some point. (1961, p. 154) A group that is dominated by attention can suddenly shift off-purpose and disperse their energies onto a new pseudo-purpose. The opposite can also be true, however; a group dominated by distraction always has the potential to rediscover or redefine its purpose and to get back on track.

In the story described here it is even possible that the shift to distraction may have helped the overall process. Once it had been spotted— through its reported impact in the other room—the group had to acknowledge their desire to hurt the other partner. They had certainly experienced *his* desire to hurt *them* but now they recognised that their own anger also left them wanting to inflict revenge on him.

Although this was only a minor incident—maybe twenty minutes in around twelve hours of negotiation—it illustrates several issues. First, it shows how swift the shift to distraction can be, and how difficult it can be to spot. Robert's awareness of Bion's ideas allowed him to notice the way in which the conversation suggested that the group purpose might have changed. They seemed to have forgotten or put to one side the real purpose and were instead "behaving as if they were acting on a basic assumption". (Bion, 1961, p. 101) They had not only "taken on" or "adopted" the new purpose but had also "taken it for granted without question as true", as if it were the real purpose. The negotiation turned abruptly into seeking revenge for past hurts. When a group is in a distracted state the real purpose is replaced by a new pseudo-purpose, which is then acted upon unquestioningly—a response that Bion characterised as "involuntary", "instantaneous", "spontaneous", "unconscious", and "instinctive". (ibid, pp. 116, 136, 153)

Second, the story highlights the potentially destructive impact of distraction. In this instance, the group managed to draw back and return to the task as soon as they recognised what they were doing. Had they insisted, however, it is easy to see how they could then have taken the other partner's aggrieved reaction as evidence that he was the one who was being difficult and unreasonable (which he was at times). He, on the other hand, would have had fresh ammunition to support his conviction that it was his ex-partner who was being unreasonable. Disagreement on this one point might have escalated and wrecked the significant progress that had been made.

Third, the incident is a reminder that distraction is inevitable. However intently a group may try to stay on track, the emotional pressures and tensions which cause distraction are always present and can quite simply become too much to bear. However, it also shows the way in which vigilant attention to the purpose can reveal such moments of slippage. Watchfulness makes it possible to "probe the reciprocal influence of the two levels of mentality operating within the group and what may be shaping this." (Armstrong, 2005, p. 146) It is even possible for moments of distraction to perform a helpful role by prompting the group to recall and restate their purpose.

Finally, it is important to note that there is a counter-intuitive side to the experience of these two kinds of thinking. As a result of the more or less instinctive way in which we tend to label things as good or bad, positive or negative, it is easy to think of attention as good and distraction as bad and to assume that attention feels good while distraction feels bad. However, the example of the negotiation reflects the flavour of distraction and attention in the moment. It shows that the relationship between the feelings associated with these two ways of thinking is neither simple nor obvious. When the negotiations were on track, the work often felt difficult, slow, and demanding, but when the group mentality switched to revenge—that is, to distraction—things suddenly seemed to move quickly and felt easier and lighter and there were smiles and some laughter: for a moment it felt good. This reversal does make sense if we recognise that the whole point of distraction is to make a difficult situation feel better. The point is that it can only do so for as long as the real purpose is kept out of mind.

In place of any value-judgment, Bion argued that the two states of mind just *are*. Both are always present, in potential at least, in all groups even though one will be dominant at any specific moment. It is only the desire for an easier group life that makes us want a solution in the form of a simple good-bad answer.

CHAPTER THREE

Truth

The need of truth is more sacred than any other need. Yet it is never mentioned.

—*Simone Weil*, 1986, p. 117

We use the term attention as a short-hand for a complex process that includes both an evenly suspended or contemplative state of mind, open to what may be important but is not yet known, and a more concentrated focus on the matter in hand, the more everyday sense of "paying attention". Consequently, the work of attention is concerned with questions and the unknown as much as with answers and the known. This complex process is guided by the pursuit of truth, the desire to work with the reality of the present moment.

In focusing on the pursuit of truth and the desire to work with reality, we are highlighting the aspirational nature of the work of attention. We are using the term truth in the same sense that the term "True" in "True North" indicates the direction of the earth's North Pole; that is, true in the sense of conforming accurately to reality. The work of attention is based on the desire to gain a true perception of things as they really are. By contrast groups are distracted from the pursuit of truth when they cannot withstand the pressures to disperse their energies into alternative emotions, thoughts, or actions. As T. S. Eliot put it, "human kind/Cannot bear very much reality". (1935, p. 190)

The work of attention in groups is founded on two convictions. First, that at any moment there is indeed a reality to be sought, which we refer to as truth *in the moment*; and second, that humans are truth-seeking beings. As the philosopher Josef Pieper put it, "human beings nourish themselves on the truth; … anyone at all who desires to live as a human is dependent on this nourishment." (1981, p. 143 [translated for this edition]) If this is right, as Bion also believed it to be, then truth is worth pursuing, however remote or inaccessible it may seem. Engaging in the pursuit of truth makes an important difference to group members' ability to work on what they are meeting to do.

One of the most challenging aspects of the pursuit of truth is that, at some level, the truth always remains essentially unknown and unknowable. As we pursue truth through attention to reality we will be affected by it even though it can never be fully experienced, let alone grasped. We can receive insights, fragments of knowledge, that allow us to understand our situation differently and to a degree more accurately. We have a problem when we become convinced that these insights represent truth itself. Truth does not give itself up in this way. Therefore, to settle on an answer as "*the* answer" is the antithesis of attention to the truth of the present moment.

Later in the chapter we will explain these ideas in more detail, but we begin with a story that is intended to give the flavour of the experience of the pursuit of truth.

> It was a cold February morning—but in a warm café in Bath—the final day of a three-day writing retreat we had allowed ourselves. When we met that morning we did not start with the agenda we had planned at the end of the previous day. This is typical of how we work together—and, indeed, of many work groups, which have a period of chatting before getting on with things. Over the years, we have learned that although this period of seemingly random conversation can distract us from the work, this is generally not the case: it can be the work. We have found that such chatting has the potential to take us deeper and more creatively into the issues that are on our agenda, often making us realise that we had conceived of them in too simplistic a way, perhaps with only a vague sense of their underlying

complexity. One result can be that an issue we had thought would be very time-consuming can be dealt with quickly and easily—or vice versa.

On this particular day we talked about many things, more or less book-related. Then Robert brought up a story he thought Peter had told him—though it turned out he had not—about a local church group that was trying to sort out a problem with the weekly flower rota. Robert finished the story by relating it to Bion's ideas and suggesting it might be suitable for inclusion in the book. He was taken aback, however, to find that Peter's interpretation of the story was entirely different to his and immediately felt incompetent and rather stupid, although he did not say so until later. On his part, Peter was confused: how could Robert have seen things the way he did? The conversation became focused on how to make sense of the story: What was right? What was wrong? How could we know the truth of what happened? Could Bion's ideas help our understanding? What did his theory really mean? We used different arguments and different rhetorical devices as each tried to persuade the other (and himself!) what the truth of the matter really was.

Eventually, we recognised the by then rather obvious fact that there was no way we could know which of us had the "right" interpretation. What had seemed an entertaining and rather simple story had turned out to be complex and involved so that both interpretations now seemed equally plausible.

We are convinced that learning to work effectively in a group means accepting that the experience is often as messy, frustrating, and inconclusive as this conversation was. It can be chaotic and can even feel like a complete failure, sometimes particularly in the period running up to what then turns out to be a significant breakthrough or moment of insight. Being conscious of the value of the search for truth is most helpful in situations where we are wrestling with intellectually challenging and emotionally demanding issues—the kind of situations, in fact, that simply may not have an easy or immediate solution and that some groups consequently choose to avoid.

Our discussion of the church flower rota brought home to us just how often our ambition when working in groups is to get to an answer. However, the pursuit of truth demands openness to the reality of the moment; it involves trying to see things as they are rather than trying to find the kind of answer that only works if we ignore the more awkward aspects of reality. When we do manage to see things as they are then answers can emerge, but often in unexpected ways which may or may not look like the answers or outcomes we thought we were seeking. For example, our discussion of how we might use the flower rota story in the book has contributed to the writing of this chapter but we have dropped the story itself.

Finding clarity in the midst of confusion

The café conversation demonstrates how messy and confusing the experience of working in groups can be. An apparently simple story about a local church group seemed at first to have an equally simple explanation but proved on reflection to be far more complex. We noticed how our attempt to get at the truth had an impact on the quality of our interaction, with our feelings swinging back and forth from confidence to incompetence, from certainty to uncertainty, and between competition and collaboration. The experience was challenging enough in a comfortable café in an apparently pleasant conversation between friends, but the sense of mess and confusion can be greatly magnified in the less comfortable and more pressured environment of the workplace, where groups are diverse, may not get on well, and often face challenging time pressures and performance measures.

The anxiety such pressures can generate is sufficient to explain why many groups choose to shy away from attending to the reality of their experience in the moment. In order to "evade frustration" (Bion, 1994, pp. 99–101) group members often fall back on tried and tested patterns that offer comfort and certainty. In addition, many people work in environments where what matters most is to find an answer or outcome. Not so for Bion. For him, it was the truth, or at least getting closer to the truth, that was most important—on the assumption, based on his experience of working with groups and individuals, that valuable developments or transformations can then arise. The capacity for attention is central to the pursuit of truth. To give attention to the truth or reality of a situation requires space, time, and mental energy because truth is always new in every moment: "attention and vigilance presuppose continuous concentration on the present moment, which must be lived as if it were, simultaneously, the first and last moment of life". (Hadot, 1995, p. 131)

In Chapter One, we told the story of Stephanie and described how she managed to keep her attention on the truth as she saw it, despite considerable pressure from her colleagues to accept an answer that had worked for a previous client in a different market—a quite different reality. Attention to the truth of her experience in the moment led her to a question not an answer, but voicing the question was in itself enough to loosen up the group's thinking, even if only temporarily.

The following story of a consultancy intervention by Peter also illustrates a difficult moment when, in the midst of confusion, what made the difference was attention to truth in the moment.

I had been asked to work with a group of eight middle managers who had been given responsibility for planning their organisation's annual management conference. This was a significant task previously undertaken by senior managers. This year, however, the chief executive had decided to delegate the planning to this group. He wanted them to design and manage a two-day residential conference with the title "Managing Organisational Change" for the company's eighty senior and middle managers. They were to be provided with support, including the guidance of the chief executive himself and my services as a consultant.

At the first meeting the discussion was frenetic. Some creative and thoughtful ideas were put forward but quickly dismissed as having already failed in the past. Those who had been energised soon became frustrated, while those who had all along been more critical felt confirmed in their cynicism. The levels of anxiety within the group increased noticeably during the morning alongside aggression, frustration, and a growing sense of apathy: the group was becoming stuck.

It was not immediately clear to me how to help these managers engage more positively with each other and with the task. Their inexperience in organising an event of this kind was obvious. In contrast, I had considerable experience of this type of activity and was tempted to take on an expert role. However, I had not been employed to organise the conference but to consult to the group to whom the task had been delegated. So I was in the same boat as the group: we did not know how to do what we were there to do. I therefore had to work hard to resist my growing desire to intervene and to tell them what I knew rather than sticking with what I did not know.

In the event I kept my ideas about conference planning to myself. I concentrated instead on taking in the experience of the group and reflecting on what I saw, heard, and felt.

After a time I began to realise that there was a shared but unrecognised confusion about the task itself. I noticed this first in the way group members were using two similar terms, "conference" and "workshop", interchangeably to describe the event and aspects of their experience from previous years. Eventually I concluded that something significant was being missed and intervened: "It seems that you may not be clear about what's expected of you in organising this management conference. In particular, I have noticed that you use the words conference and workshop as if they're just the same thing—but at the same time you make sound as if a 'conference' is all about providing answers, whereas your experience of workshops at previous events seems to have a more exploratory feel to it—people working on issues together and sharing their experiences, difficulties, insights, and so on." This comment seemed to settle the anxiety for a moment and to stimulate a more measured discussion.

Quite quickly the group concluded that there was no way their annual conference could hope to provide answers because the organisation was right in the middle of a large-scale change process and "in such a mess" as one of them put it. At the same time, they recognised that they had all assumed that the task they had been given was to organise a conference that would come up with answers. No wonder they were getting more and more anxious. My observation enabled them to get more in touch with the emotional reality in the group and the terrifying reality of being responsible for solving the impossible. They began to reflect on what a management conference could realistically be expected to achieve, dropped the impossible expectation, and sought to design a conference with the aim of "providing participants with a range of opportunities to meet and to explore important issues together". They later revealed that the clarification of the task of the planning meeting had been a significant step forward in their work.

What caught Peter's attention in this case was the sense of "stuckness". The group seemed to be going around in circles with no way of escaping the growing atmosphere of frustration, cynicism, and anger at what was being expected of them.

Peter was alerted to the truth of what was happening in this group by a growing sense of frustration and by the recognition of a desire to provide an answer—as an "expert". The pressure he felt to come out of role matched the enormous pressure they were experiencing to come up with a solution. The uncontained emotion had divided the group members' attention: some were still thinking about the event while some started acting out old rivalries and others tried to find someone to blame for all of this—notably the chief executive for giving them the task in the first place.

In situations like this it is sometimes possible to help group members to refocus their attention by simply reminding them of what they are meeting to do: "This is all very well but isn't the group supposed to be …?" Others may then recognise what is going on and redirect their energies back onto the task in hand. However, misdirected attention can make it impossible for group members to see that they have lost touch with their intended purpose. They become convinced that there are other issues that need to be worked out: is there someone to blame for the difficulties we are experiencing? Is the chief executive just using this as a test for future promotions? Are old rivals in the group trying to put me down? A sense that we are already doing what we are there to do can make it impossible to listen to anyone suggesting otherwise, and the intensity of the experience makes it seem obvious that we are right and the individual voice is wrong. The belief that "we are victims/being tested/being attacked" provides a certain comfort which may be preferable to acknowledging that we do not know how to do what we are here to do.

In this instance, Peter felt under enormous pressure to take up a knowing position where he would just tell them how to organise the conference. However, awareness of this pressure in the moment made it possible for him to stay with the experience of not-knowing without rushing in to ease their obvious discomfort and frustration. He waited long enough for an idea to form that offered some insight into the situation. Although the intervention did not present an answer, it raised a question group members were able to engage with and seemed to offer sufficient containment for them to remember the task that they were meeting to do.

It is worth noting the specifics of this intervention as an illustration of one way in which attention to the truth or reality of the moment can be enacted. What came to his aid was attention to the particular use of language in the group. In our experience the way words are used can offer a way in, especially if one is ready to accept that language can be used as much to obscure as to enlighten. (Bion, 1970, p. 3) Words can help us to manage our anxieties by giving the appearance of knowing, when in reality the reason for our anxiety is that we do not know. This is more than likely to be the case if the challenge facing the group is to engage with a new situation rather than to remember an old answer. Inevitably the group will recognise at some point that it does not know what it is doing. Silence is probably a helpful strategy as it can create time to think. However, in the panic of uncertainty, some group members are likely to start talking more—filling the empty space as a way of feeling less anxious and, more often than not, using familiar words or stories from the past rather than holding onto the unfamiliar in the moment.

In this case, Peter's intervention met the group members where they were: not castigating them for their behaviour but attempting to find a connection between their defensive, misdirected state and the truth of a moment, which in their current state of not knowing was just too challenging for them to sustain. Descriptive categories such as "conference" and "workshop" can be important markers of both the group purpose and the dominant way of working; drawing attention to them can make a difference. This was an experienced group of women and men and they quickly saw that the way they were using these words was important. It enabled them to recognise their state of mind and their more or less unconscious motivations—and then to do something about it.

Another feature of the interaction is worth noting. As consultant, Peter managed to hold onto his sense of role. This may be understood as retaining clarity about the relationship between his purpose and the group's—between what the group was meeting to do and why Peter was there. He experienced considerable pressure to give them answers, to demonstrate that they could rely on him. Of course he could see what was *not* happening, as could they, but he did not have a solution to hand. In other words, Peter experienced a pressure to enact with them a form of dependency that could so easily have undermined the chief executive in his attempt to delegate responsibility to this group. By not getting caught up in what almost amounted to panic in the group, Peter was able to go on thinking, to resist the pressure to collude, to notice the uncertainty, contradiction, and defensiveness in their use of language, and finally to formulate a comment which drew attention to it. Attention can breed attention just as distraction divides and disperses it.

The greater the uncertainty in a group, the more helpful it can be to have in mind an approach based on attention to truth in the moment. There is no guarantee that it will resolve the uncertainty, but when everything else seems to be in flux it can at least give something to hold onto and help to find clarity in the midst of confusion. Our conversation in the café shows how working in a group can seem to be going nowhere—and of course sometimes these conversations of ours do not go anywhere and we just have to give up. However, more often than not we have found that by attending not just to the content of the discussion but also to the reality of our interactions in the moment—our anger or sense of anxiety, incompetence, and competition—we get to a place where we see or understand things differently.

We have tried, in the two stories we have told so far in this chapter, to give an idea of what it can feel like to attend to truth in the moment. While it is likely at one level to be frustrating, faith in the approach can also contain anxieties that might otherwise be disabling—"contain anxiety in a manner conducive to growth". (Emanuel, 2001, p. 1072) In this way, it can be possible to continue despite the discomfort of not knowing, in the belief that an intuition of the truth may emerge. The intuition that emerges may take the form of a question rather than an answer, but this can be the basis for progress no matter how tentative.

When insights of this kind emerge they can be surprising and energising—and even fun: a reward for sticking with the discomfort, confusion, or annoyance. This is particularly true when the work is important and has the potential to make a real difference. Behind the strong, apparently negative emotions there often lies a sense of not knowing what is going on. And even if we think we do know what is happening then we may not know how to intervene or even how to just *be* in the group in a way that is helpful and satisfying. Attention to the pursuit of truth in the moment can help us not to react to this uncertainty by turning our backs on it and retreating into tried-and-tested, known patterns of behaviour. If we can do this then we have a chance of achieving something interesting. It all depends on having ways of managing our fears and anxieties sufficiently well to allow us to continue thinking and to keep going. A key first step may be to trust Armstrong's insight that emotional experience of all kinds can be a source of learning rather than something to be avoided or suppressed.

Truth is essential for human development

> There is never an authentic disclosure of truth which is not also transformative.
>
> (Tracy, 1981, cited in Burton-Christie, 1993, p. 32)

Any insight, no matter how small, into what is *really* going on in a group—that is, into truth in the moment—can be transformational. This is the case whether it concerns the relationships between group members, their relationship to the group purpose, or the nature of interactions with others outside the group. Insight into truth of this kind is not the same as knowledge. Even if no one knows what is actually happening, the reality of the moment is critically important to the working of a group. It is through the search for truth that knowledge can be acquired and, as Tracy says in the phrase above that echoes Bion's insights, an authentic disclosure of truth is always transformative.

This relationship between truth and knowing is crucial to the experience of working in groups, but it is complex. There is, for example, the relationship between truth and un-truth; also between knowing and not-knowing; and there is "hidden" knowledge—not necessarily a lie (Armstrong, 2005, pp. 10–28) but something that, because it is known to one person and not to others, can cause a problematic gap in understanding. The following story illustrates just how different the truth can seem from different perspectives:

> The new manager of a professional group sought to introduce the disciplines of project reporting by requiring all team members to provide a weekly, written update on each of their client engagements. He chose to introduce this because he believed group members were not working well enough together. Among other things, they seemed to him to lack coordination, the capacity to learn from experience, and problem-solving capabilities.
>
> However, several members of the group resisted the changes and were persistently tardy in completing their reports. As a consequence, the manager and other members of the team felt aggrieved that they

were not being kept fully informed of developments in the projects led by these group members.

The resistant group members held a somewhat different view. They did not entirely trust the manager's stated motivation and believed he was seeking to undermine their professional autonomy in order to gain power and to control both them and their projects, for which some felt an almost parental sense of ownership and protectiveness. Whilst they acknowledged that the request seemed reasonable and may have been innocuous, they could not see why these reporting requirements had any real benefit for project performance. Their view was that the best way to improve all the problems the manager had identified would be through open discussion at their regular team meetings. They argued that the reporting regime was an additional demand upon their already overloaded working day. More importantly, they also felt that if they acceded to these demands then it would create a shift in power relations that might later be exploited.

Other more emotionally difficult layers to the differences within the group were voiced by one individual, who believed that the strength of the emotional reaction to the introduction of the new reporting regime indicated a deeper level of disturbance. He feared it was just one instance of a broader issue that could not be acknowledged, let alone discussed head-on. He thought the scheme was relatively unimportant in itself but also described it as "the thin end of the wedge" and a "Trojan horse". He saw it as a way of disguising the reality that their professional culture, which he believed was the organisation's strength and had been the reason he had joined it and stayed, was now under attack from a new class of young managers who may have studied management but knew nothing about the actual work.

We were presented here with several interpretations, all of which appeared plausible but we did not know which one was right. Our assumption was that they were all partial and that the most fruitful way forward would be to find a safe way for each party to disclose their understanding of the situation to the other. At such moments, questioning and dialogue can exemplify the approach we are describing here. Rather than defending fixed positions, it can encourage those involved to attend to the individual experience of how the new scheme is affecting them in the moment. As a result, more or less hidden assumptions can be brought to light, which can enable a deeper understanding of the problem.

Bion seems to have been particularly gifted in spotting moments of this kind. They reflect a deep-rooted conflict in human nature: the fact that we both want to know and want not to know, or do not want to do the work required to grapple with what we do not know. He described this vividly in relation to ideas in the field of psychoanalysis: "We learn these theories—Freud's, Jung's, Klein's—and try to get them absolutely rigid so as to avoid having to do any more thinking." (1978, p. 6) The basis for the conflict is an innate tension between the pursuit of truth and the forces opposed to it: To know or not to know? To seek or to evade the truth? To go on thinking or to turn a blind eye? Again and again, Bion put his finger on this raw spot.

However, the power of truth to initiate development is also based on an apparently contradictory tension: although there is always a truth to be found in the moment it is always partial and temporary—true for an instant, an hour, a week, a year, but not for ever. Any insight into the truth of the situation actually alters the situation—and the result of disclosing one truth may be that now there is another layer of truth to be found.

Questions and answers

In the context of his work as a psychoanalyst, it is not hard to understand Bion's commitment to the search for truth. After all, analyst and patient are trying to uncover truths hidden under habits of thinking and acting, which may be holding the patient back. However, Bion applied this principle more widely, arguing that the quest for truth is fundamental to all human development and suggesting that *all* emotional growth is underpinned by the drive to seek and know the truth: "truth seems to be essential for psychic growth". (1962, p. 56) This has led Grotstein to suggest that Bion was pointing to the existence of a "truth drive" or "instinct" at the heart of the human personality. (Grotstein, 2004, 2007)

Using the same image as Josef Pieper, quoted at the start of this chapter, Bion observed that just as malnutrition can deform the body, so too can humans remain mentally and emotionally stunted when starved of the truth: "healthy mental growth seems to depend on truth as the living organism depends on food". (1965, p. 38) He was, however, under no illusions about the ever present temptation to avoid the challenge of the new and instead "always to engage upon something familiar". (1990, p. 5) He fought against "the bigotry of certitude", (1991, p. 34) describing our attraction to the forces opposed to the pursuit of truth as a craving:

> There is always a craving to slap in an answer so as to prevent any spread of the flood through the gap which exists. Experience brings it home to you that you can give what we call "answers" but they are really space stoppers. It is a way of putting an end to curiosity—especially if you can succeed in believing the answer is *the* answer. Otherwise you widen the breach, this nasty hole where one hasn't any knowledge at all. (1978, p. 22)

This gap or space—"this nasty hole where one hasn't any knowledge at all"—is the place of ignorance. However, we only think of ignorance as nasty if we feel disturbed rather than stimulated by it. Its impact is of course likely to be greater in a group because of the way any emotional disturbance experienced by the individual tends to be magnified through force of numbers, and also through a certain sense of guilt or responsibility: the feeling that I/we "*should*" know.

No wonder then that Bion described the group situation, "whatever it may appear to be on the surface", as "charged with emotions which exert a powerful, and frequently unobserved, influence on the individual." He added that, as a result, "his emotions are stirred to the detriment of his judgment". (1961, pp. 39–40) It is the strength of these emotions that can lead to a group becoming distracted from its purpose. As group members retreat from questions and uncertainties, they replace the pursuit of truth with the search for an answer. The problem is, however, that the solutions found usually turn out to be the answer given to a previous, different question.

Finding an answer is one way to manage a question's power to disturb, but in doing so, its potential to spark development can also be dissipated or lost. This is why Bion often quoted a phrase of Maurice Blanchot's, *la réponse est le malheur de la question*: "the answer is the misfortune or disease of curiosity—it kills it"; "If you have any curiosity it is answers which put paid to it." (1978, pp. 21–22, 40) In a similar vein, Fink describes how the French analyst Lacan reminded his students again and again:

> … to stop trying to understand everything, because understanding is ultimately a form of defence, of bringing everything back to what

is already known. The more you try to understand, the less you hear—the less you can hear something new and different. (Fink, 1996, cited in Snell, 2013, p. 58)

For Bion, not knowing and the questions that emerge from it need to be thought of differently—not defined as negative just because they are so often experienced as unsettling. Provided that group members are able to contain disturbing emotions without being thrown by them, then not knowing can also represent a potentially creative space. His spatial metaphor is reflected in everyday phrases such as "narrow-minded", "broad-minded", and "open-minded".

Any question, however apparently trivial or superficial, can be an expression of the pursuit of truth and has the power to stimulate development at some level—to broaden the mind and increase the capacity for attention. The word question is, after all, derived from the Latin verb *quaerere* meaning "to look or search for". So the potential for development is right there at every moment, but whether or not it is realised depends on the quality of our attention and on our capacity to remain open to truth in the moment. Mark Cocker captures the issue very neatly in describing our capacity to respond to beauty in the natural world: "A really significant element in ascribing beauty to a thing lies not within itself, but in the quality of our attention to it." (Cocker, 2007, p. 42)

In every line of work there is a tendency to look for and value people who *know*. These are the people we typically think of as doing a good job and, of course, this is right and good. However, to work effectively in groups also demands the capacity to perform our roles when we do not know. What has come to shape our work with groups, therefore, is not so much the demand for answers but rather attention to the nature of the questions asked. New learning occurs at the edges between known and un-known, or in the tension between what is known but is also denied, avoided, or otherwise defended against—between the desire to know and resistance to knowing.

The pressure to know

We would like to end this chapter with a final story. It describes a moment when Marianne became acutely aware of the tensions we have been describing between the pressure from others to come up with an answer and her own need to know more about what was really going on. It occurred when she was working as head of year in a large, mixed comprehensive school.

> One morning, a group of unusually bright and self-confident sixteen year old students arrived in Marianne's office at break time with a complaint about one of their teachers. And then, during the lunch break on the same day, this same teacher arrived with a complaint about the group and about one student in particular.
>
> This student could be more challenging than most but generally speaking in an appropriate way. She was intelligent, well-read, and politically aware, and could always be relied on to stimulate discussion in any group. She was also attractive and vivacious and something of a leader among her peers, socially as well as intellectually. On leaving school she worked for some time as a fashion model. The teacher was a middle-aged male and quite opinionated but in a way that inspired and brought out the best in many male students while irritating many females.
>
> The pressure Marianne experienced in both meetings was that although everyone appeared to have come to her with questions, all they really wanted was an answer. It was also clear that both sides knew what that answer should be: for the group it was to get rid of the teacher, for the teacher it was to get rid of this particular student or to control her so that she would stop poisoning the group and spoiling it for everyone. The problem was being framed, as so often in schools but also in organisations more generally, as a personality clash.
>
> Something had to be done. Marianne had to intervene in some way. However, it was also clear that for a variety of reasons neither the group's nor the teacher's answers were adequate. She also sensed that some kind of creative solution was necessary but that to find it she would have to withstand, for a while at least, the pressure on her to provide the answer. Any answer that came from outside the actual classroom situation would be likely to leave any broader issues untouched only to resurface in another form at a later date.

When she told us about this series of events, Marianne described how rather than just reacting, she had slowed down, partly because she knew she needed a moment's pause, and partly because she just did not know what to think, let alone what to do. She also said just how unusual it was for her to allow herself to pause like this because her role meant that she felt constantly under pressure to solve other people's problems for them, immediately.

In this pause for reflection Marianne recognised that there may indeed have been an element of personality clash between the two individuals involved, but she also assumed that this was unlikely to be the only issue that might need to be dealt with. As she thought the whole thing through, a series of questions began to emerge: Why now—and why on the same day? What, if anything, did the focus on the older man and the young woman say about gender relations in this group and in her year group more generally, and maybe even in the school as a whole? What were the implications for her in her role as the only female head of year in the school? What was the role of other senior colleagues, in particular the head of the subject department involved and the other staff in his department? Was there a danger that the apparent clash between these two individuals would deflect attention away from a more hidden conflict of some kind—between different approaches to learning, for instance, or between different understandings of staff and student roles and responsibilities? Were there, as she suspected, also issues of class and power lurking behind the more obvious issues of age, gender, and possibly sexuality? And in what ways might any intervention on her part either support or undermine learning and development, intellectual and personal, not only within this specific group but also in the year group and the school more broadly?

This example underlines the importance of sticking with questions and not rushing to close the awkward gap created by not knowing. Attending to truth in the moment can take many forms: taking seriously the tension between knowing and not knowing; recognising the speed with which we *stop* thinking; accepting the conflict between the desire for truth and resistance to facing the truth; or acknowledging how, despite our intention to keep an open mind, we nonetheless find ourselves dispersing our energies into activity, explanations, or emotional reactions because of the apparent comfort they can provide.

CHAPTER FOUR

Cooperation

> The problem that confronts us today … is how to be one's self and yet in oneness with others, to feel deeply with all human beings and yet retain one's own characteristic qualities.

—*Goldman*, 1917, p. 267

In *Experiences in Groups*, Bion introduced the strange term "groupishness" to highlight a fundamental aspect of being human. Hinshelwood has described this as one of Bion's "obscure pieces of common sense" (2008, p. 72). Although the word only appears three times in the book, the idea reverberates throughout. On the first occasion, he uses it to describe the individual's "inalienable quality as a herd animal" (Bion, 1961, p. 95) and also to convey the discomfort individuals can experience as a result of this quality. On the second and third occasions, he repeats the same sentence almost word for word in a discussion of the relationship between group and individual psychology: "The individual is a group animal at war, both with the group and with those aspects of his personality that constitute his 'groupishness.'" (ibid., p. 168; see also p. 131)

Bion held the view that group psychology and individual psychology are not independent fields because the individual is always a group member, whether geographically alone or in a group: "there are characteristics in the individual whose real significance cannot be understood unless it is realised that they are part of his equipment as a herd animal". (Ibid., p. 133) He challenges the dominant modern notion of the human being as a skin-encapsulated ego arguing that "the individual is, and always has been, a member of a group". (Ibid., p. 168)

It may have been his focus on the pathological manifestations of group dynamics that led Bion to use the language of warfare to describe our relationship to these two sides of our nature. Conflicts in our external relationships to actual groups are often obvious, whereas internal conflicts, stemming from the fact that we are both drawn to and repelled by group membership, are subtle and complex but no less real or disturbing.

However, warfare is not the only consequence of our groupishness. Distractions exist in all groups but positive dynamics also arise when attention dominates the mentality of the group. This positive dimension to the experience of groupishness may be better described as "cooperation", a word Bion also used to capture times when individual and group purposes are in alignment (e.g., Ibid., pp. 11, 98, 116, 177). This experience is complementary to, and always co-exists in potential with, the experience of being a group animal at war.

Despite its apparent simplicity, the idea that the individual is a group animal masks a deeply complex dimension of what it means to be human. Bion is expressing a paradox: the individual is both identifiably separate and essentially social, that is, inseparable from others. It is an inescapable tension in human nature that constantly generates inner and outer conflict. Alford paraphrased Bion's image:

> The enemy is not just the group. The enemy is our own desire to give ourselves over to the group. Unlike real enemies, this enemy can never be defeated. At best we can live with it, but first we have to know it. (2004, p. 7)

However real the conflict may be between individuals within the group or with other groups, it also reflects or expresses conflicts in the inner world of each group member. As a result, neither side can ever be victorious, although there may be truces, breaks in the hostilities, or periods of relative peace when one side is dominant and the other submissive or, more creatively, when the two sides cooperate on the basis of a common cause.

So our groupishness is not a stable state but rather an aspect of human togetherness. We are constantly subject to the dynamic tensions that arise from this split affiliation between the individual part of ourselves and the group or social part. Each of us identifies in ourselves an "I" and a "we", a "me" and an "us", and the priority we give to one or the other is subject to fluctuation at any moment.

> To be an individual in the group and to know oneself as such requires a subtle and difficult balance of merger and differentiation, in which the individual is at once a part of the group, merged with it, and at the same time valued and recognised for his or her difference. (Alford, 1994, p. 40)

This basic tension cannot be resolved by just opting for one's own preferred mode—individual-self or group-self—because we need both our separateness and our togetherness. As a result, we experience simultaneously various feelings that may be in conflict. The positive aspects cannot be kept apart from the negative, "cannot be experienced except in fixed combination with other less desired and often strongly disliked feelings". (Bion, 1961, p. 95) So while groupishness cannot be classified as good or bad—it just *is*—there is no doubt that it adds to the complexity of experience. It is because our cooperation in the group is rooted in our groupishness that both elements require our attention.

Institutional conflict and cooperation

The following story describes how an attempted collaboration between two university departments had come to be so dominated by distraction that it had become almost impossible to work together. However, it demonstrates how attention can encourage cooperation. In this case, hostile interactions that were characterised by rivalry and conflict eventually gave way to a constructive engagement in which individual members came to work together cooperatively in a way that was in everyone's interests.

> Rebecca had only recently taken over the leadership of a group which was supposed to be cooperating on a project with a group in another

faculty in the university. It was immediately obvious, however, that far from working together the two groups were totally at logger-heads. A lot of energy was being expended but the hoped-for partnership was in reality stagnating.

The purpose of the collaboration was to deliver a shared master's degree programme, but it quickly became clear to Rebecca that her predecessor had pressed ahead to establish the programme despite stiff resistance within her own faculty. Although the new degree had run with small numbers for two years, considerable tensions had also developed. This was reflected, for example, in the fact that during a short period of time three different programme managers had been appointed.

The behaviour of those involved quickly demonstrated some of the underlying difficulties: individuals storming out of meetings, the refusal of people on both sides to talk to members of the other faculty, tears, absences from meetings, angry emails, and so on. As you might expect, different individuals were blamed for the problems depending on who you talked to. The only consistent message from both sides was that it was the fault of the other faculty.

At the start, Rebecca also found herself caught up in the fantasy that she needed to sort out the fight before the real purpose could be addressed. Eventually, however, she came to the conclusion that any attempts to do so were futile, so she simply stopped trying. She was aware that her reaction was more or less instinctive, even defensive, in the sense that she just wanted to stop wasting so much time. However, a few months later she was surprised to realise that she had begun to develop a good working relationship with her equivalent in the other faculty. They had started to collaborate effectively on other inter-faculty projects, which successfully combined the strengths of both. Their working relationship was increasingly relaxed and they were able to talk freely about problems as they arose.

Eventually they turned their attention to the problematic master's programme and decided to give it another try. The joint programme managers from both faculties were invited to a review meeting, which turned out to be open and good-natured leading to a free and direct exchange of ideas. Within half an hour the agenda had shifted radically from reviewing the current programme to planning a significant redesign.

The proposals from this meeting were taken to senior managers within the respective faculties, who quickly gave their support. In time for the next academic year, a new degree had been designed, validated, and marketed with such success that it immediately became one of the largest postgraduate programmes in the two faculties. The fighting, scapegoating, and name-calling diminished and lost its edge, although without disappearing altogether. Bi-monthly meetings of senior managers from both faculties were established to review and progress the growing number of inter-faculty collaborations.

Although the situation was clearly painful for everyone, each faculty team simply exported a great deal of their pain by blaming the other. This allowed them to avoid the inevitable work that would have been required if they had looked at their own part in the fracas. By putting their energies into blaming and fighting the other group, everyone felt excused from the challenge of the actual tasks for which the partnership had been set up in the first place. It was as if the explicit purpose of collaboration had been replaced by another: fighting and winning—not losing at least—or finding a scapegoat in order to avoid being blamed oneself.

At a crucial moment, Rebecca took a step back. In doing so, she was not consciously trying to create a "space" but this enabled her to relax her focused attention and to draw instead upon a more evenly suspended attention: waiting, observing, listening, patience, watchfulness, discernment. The breakthrough came when attention was given to the potential for cooperation instead of focusing on finding a solution to what was being defined as the problem. This did not come in the form of a clear decision or dramatic insight. It was fuzzier and more unsettling than that: Rebecca simply became tired of the endless round of bickering and blame and felt that it would be a waste of time and energy and a further distraction to join the fight. Any attempt she made directly to intervene just seemed to be experienced by others as yet another attack: fighting for a solution just stoked the fires. It was the space created by withdrawing—fleeing, not fighting—that allowed proper attention to be given to what was actually going on. This meant doing something different, even if that meant doing nothing. This is not the kind of thing that is typically expected of those in leadership roles.

Shifting attention in this way cannot, of course, be expected to produce an instant solution, but in this case it did help to create the conditions for something different to happen. Without attention it seems quite likely that the situation would just have gone on as it was, making it almost inevitable that at some point either the course would have collapsed or the collaboration would have ended and one faculty would have taken over on its own.

This example shows that we cannot fully understand attention in groups unless we also understand how and why they become distracted. Admirable and useful though it may be to look at best practice, this story suggests that an indispensable part of best practice is to understand what blocks it because only then is it possible to respond effectively when things go wrong.

When its inherent tensions are held in creative balance, groupishness can provide a powerful source of satisfaction in groups. At such times, the energy of the different parts is brought together in the service of the task—ideas flow, work can become play, and thinking together is exciting, challenging, and fruitful.

The problem is that groupishness can be experienced simultaneously as both desirable and disliked and can therefore cause considerable emotional discomfort. When the tensions created are out of balance, they can become a powerful source of mental and psychic pain, undermining attention and stimulating individual and group distraction. In an attempt to feel better we tend to split one part off from the other, thereby isolating ourselves externally from the group and internally from this perplexing part of ourselves that needs both; that is, we favour only one aspect our "essential 'groupishness'". (Bion, 1961, p. 95)

In part therefore, the complexity of the group setting arises from the fact that the focus of our attention shifts between individual and group, or between the group and individual aspects of our personality, sometimes seeing both but more often losing one altogether. It is hard to keep both perspectives in mind at the same time. However, the phrase "keep both perspectives in mind" makes it sound like just one choice among others. It does not convey the emotional tone of an experience, which might be better expressed in Faust's anguished cry, early in Goethe's play: "Two souls, alas, are housed within my breast!" (1949, p. 67) While the "souls" being explored by Goethe and Bion are not the same, the pain caused by an irresolvable tension of this kind can be of just this order.

The individual and the group

Born into a group—the family—we are from the outset deeply dependent upon cooperating with those around us. We generally feel separate and look separate, with individual passports, driving licences, and exam certificates, and a constant encouragement to be independent. However strong the pull to separation may be, we also need to cooperate with one another to meet our needs: from the basics of food, water, and reproduction, to transport, computers, and education. Even when we are on our own we carry others with us—our families, friendship groups, school and work groups, ethnic, social, and community groups, gender and age groups.

The depth of our need for cooperation is clearly reflected in the way we learn to speak. Language is an essentially group phenomenon. For example, so-called feral children who did not learn to speak before they went wild and spent their formative years away from human groupings, are unable to pick up speech beyond single or small groups of words. (Newton, 2002) And none of us just learns the standard form of our first language: we learn the dialect which is spoken in "our" group, often learning to adapt our accent and the registers of language we use to fit with the particular language group we are with—at work, at home, with friends, and so on.

Emotionally, however, it can be hard to stay in touch with the two sides of the paradoxical reality of groupishness. We are caught between our dependence on the group and our independence of it, between our need and desire to be alone and our need and desire for belonging and for membership. It is as intimate to us as the air we breathe and the words we use—so familiar indeed that it is easy to ignore and to convince ourselves either that we are on our own or instead that we cannot be.

As a result, being in a group can be rather like being unable to see the wood for the trees. You can see the individual in the group but it is hard to see the group in the individual—or to put it the other way round, you can take the individual out of the group but you cannot take the group out of the individual. This becomes evident when former soldiers are interviewed and are often so overcome with grief that they cannot speak about lost comrades whether just eight hours or eighty years later. The group to which they were attached is clearly still so vividly present to them—or rather, present in them—that the years simply fall away. "At the going down of the sun and in the morning, we will remember them." (Binyon, 1914) This does not suggest an effort of willpower; it is a statement of fact, a simple recognition of inseparability: at all times of day and night, in every waking and sleeping moment, you, our group and our individual comrades and friends, will be present to us. "Remember" means "recall to mind" but here it also suggests re-"membering": putting the members of a body, the group, back together.

Despite the fact that much of the time the tensions of groupishness and the complexities of cooperation are not visible, there are moments when it can become obvious. For example, when athletes—clearly individuals, with their individual gold medals around their necks— are asked about their achievement, they often say they could not have done it alone, and then thank those who made their success possible. It is clear that they really mean it and also that it is indeed true, that "I" did it *and* "we" did it: "As athletes, it is us that stand on the podium at the end of the day, but it really is down to thousands of others …" (Peacock, 2012) Nonetheless, it is still the individual athlete, tennis player, author, musician, scientist, or peace activist who is awarded the prize. In Formula 1 racing, the tension is to some degree acknowledged by awarding points to the car constructors as well as the winning drivers. More typically, however, even in team sports where the entire team is recognised the importance of the cooperative efforts of the wider group is not—that is, the trainers, coaches, ground staff, sports psychologists, sponsors, spectators, and so on, who together make the team performance possible.

A delicate balance

The effects of groupishness are so complex and far-reaching that it is not possible to convey their scope or depth in one example. Its impact is evident, more or less explicitly, in every story that we tell. However, we would like to tell a story here in which one individual's experience at work was deeply affected by living through the impact of groupishness. The story concerns Michael's experience in a new job. For the first hundred days, the balance between his individual and social needs, and between his needs and those of the group he had joined, was good enough for him to be able to ignore the potential tensions and difficulties. From then on, however, the cracks became too wide to be papered over any longer. We will tell the story in two parts, before and after the one-hundred-day watershed.

Part 1: Days 1–100

From the start Michael loved everything about the job and everyone he met. The induction meeting seemed to set the tone. He found himself sitting next to someone whose mother was born in the same small village in the north of England that his father's family came from. They shared memories of childhood visits and of swimming in the same rivers. They had not spoken since that first day, which was a shame, but it had really helped him to get over the anxiety of not knowing anyone, making things seem somehow familiar.

Michael had had nearly a year without what he would have called a "proper" job—paying the bills and getting by thanks to a mixture of part-time shifts at the local pub and various temporary jobs, none lasting more than three months. In the search for a job that matched his aspirations, however, he found that qualifications and experience he had assumed would be "relevant" did not seem relevant enough—until, quite out of the blue, the seemingly perfect job just appeared. A chance meeting with a friend, a promised phone number that actually came through, an interview within a week, the offer of a two-year contract, and within the month the first day arrived.

The company he had joined had won a massive export contract and recruited twenty-five people within three months to cover a range of jobs, mainly in technical support and production. Michael's engineering degree was the key to getting him into the production department, even though his skills and experience did not really fit. That was okay though, as full training was provided which was actually very good, better, Michael felt, than any of his seminars at university, and the learning was directly relevant to the problems and challenges he was working on. His weekly progress meetings with his line manager were really encouraging; she was delighted with his performance.

Michael also joined the company squash club, which he enjoyed, though he was not entirely convinced it was a good thing when he beat one of the department managers in his first game. It got him noticed. In the second week, there was a social to the local Mega-Bowl, followed by pizza. A small group formed and started having lunch together—sometimes as many as seven or eight.

His immediate team was made up of eight people—six "old hands" and two "newbies". When the training finished, Michael was given more responsibility and relished the opportunity to show what he could do.

In this first part of the story, we see what appears to be a good resolution of any tensions between Michael's aspirations as an individual and the benefits of being in a group. Not only did he need the job, he enjoyed it and was intellectually stimulated and challenged by it. The group appeared to need him for who he was as an individual and for the particular blend of experience and personality that he brought both to the technical elements of the work and to the team.

It was only towards the end of the first hundred days that he began to realise he and the others who had joined with him had been experiencing a kind of honeymoon period. The joy of the honeymoon may only last a few hours or may continue for a hundred days but at some point things tend to change. At this moment Michael could no longer ignore the tension between his individual and group sides, nor the fractures it was causing. His positive experience of the work lasted a relatively long time, perhaps because of the particular blend of personalities and goodwill in the group and an unusual level of personal and political support. However, it may also have depended on turning a blind eye to certain experiences, in particular the experience of individual ↔ group tensions that may have been evident but were also masked by the fact that Michael's contract involved plenty of time away from the group, whether to travel or to work on his own for significant periods. He knew that this suited him well and it had been one element of the original job description that had caught his eye.

In the end, however, things did change.

Part 2: Day 100 to the end

Michael described the moment when the honeymoon came to an end as "a sobering experience". He knew he should have expected it but everything had started so well and he had been grateful to be given the opportunity and to be recognised for his abilities. He had done well enough at school and at university but had never excelled, never felt singled out. Here, however, his manager had taken the time to give him specific, professional feedback on a regular basis—and most of it was really positive.

The first time he noticed that things might be taking a different turn was during a meeting when he saw two of his colleagues, both old hands, sharing a private joke. He noticed it because it seemed to be about him and happened immediately after he had made a suggestion for improving their maintenance processes. He caught their glances as they laughed to themselves.

A few days later he was summoned to his manager's office. When he arrived she did not greet him with her usual warm smile—instead she looked serious. She said that he did not need to worry, there was not a serious problem, but she had received a complaint—well, not so much a complaint as some murmuring in the team. She did not want to name names but more than one person had hinted that they felt Michael was not being a team player—that he was claiming credit for ideas that were not his own. "I just want to put this in your mind so that you can reflect on things a little."

Summarily dispatched without a chance to reply, Michael walked away sick to the pit of his stomach. He had no idea what this could be about but was annoyed with his colleagues—and assumed he knew two of them at least. Even worse, he was deeply upset and angry at the way his manager had taken their side and not given him a chance to explore what this was all about.

Nothing was ever said about it again and he never again noticed them laughing after he spoke at meetings. However, he also knew that he was being less forthcoming with his ideas, and the niggle never went away; work never felt quite the same again.

Shortly after this, Michael heard on the grapevine a piece of news that suddenly seemed to make the background to the situation clearer to him. Due to changes in the company's circumstances, the long-term job prospects for the twenty-five new employees had changed radically: instead of twenty-five permanent posts being available there would only be three. Michael was shocked to discover how many of his friends were seeking work elsewhere and he too started to fill in application forms. Within the next hundred days not one of those who had joined with him was left.

From an early age we are all more or less aware of the tensions at the heart of groupishness. While things were going well Michael had chosen to forget that his feeling of independence from the group was an illusion; he knew that he could not do without the rest of the group and the wider organisation. For much of the time we have our own ways of coping with these tensions, which is why for the first hundred days Michael did not experience any real difficulties. The tension was still there; it just was not an immediate problem for him.

Thinking back, Michael realised that from the beginning he had been half aware of a certain tension in relation to the "old hands" and to his manager. He had not paid it much attention however, because he knew that the "newbies" had all come as outsiders into a relatively settled group that was having to deal with a significant change. He remembered his fleeting moment of concern at defeating the departmental manager at squash and realised it had hinted at a potential fault line in the group. He had made himself stand out and realised now that others may have felt that he had won at someone else's expense; maybe that was the origin of the whole story that he was not a team player. But then squash is not a team game.

It now began to seem as if being a team player in his work group had come to mean playing to the rules—whether you knew them or not—and conforming to a collective that pressurised individuals to fit in rather than encouraging creativity and individual skills. In the early days, he had experienced an uncomplicated movement between individuality and group membership but that balance had now tipped. After the reprimand from his manager about his behaviour in the work team, he knew what it felt like to be a team player: don't rock the boat by stepping out of line. Gone was the sense of being welcomed as a new player bringing fresh ideas to what was, in reality, a new team with a new purpose and structure, even if it did contain several "old" players.

The tensions of groupishness can remain balanced for as long as there is a good match between the needs of individuals and the group, but as external circumstances change, the fit between individual and group needs also tends to shift. In the end, the most obvious and significant change for Michael was that the organisational and group purpose no longer supported each individual's immediate need for a job.

This story is a reminder that the group ↔ individual tension is derived, in part at least, from the painfully learned experience that not everyone can be trusted and even that no one is trustworthy all of the time. As a result, our experience of groups can come to be dominated by the learned need to defend ourselves against the predicted attacks and deceit of others. This is an important aspect of learning how to survive in the world. However, if we erect these defences too well and apply them in an indiscriminate manner we can end up not only protecting ourselves from bad experiences but also shutting ourselves off from the good: we can lose touch with the innate capacity that we share for cooperation. Disturbingly this is not a description of madness, a rare event, but is an all too characteristic aspect of our normal, day-to-day experience, which deeply affects our work in groups and in society as a whole.

Every group finds its own balance between the expectations placed on individuals to align themselves with the group and to remain separate. So once again it is not that one side is right and the other wrong, however much it can feel like that. We may want to join in or do it on our own or feel we should leave or stay, but at some level we know that whichever choice we make, we always face the possibility of finding or losing ourselves. We fear the loss of our individuality by becoming totally absorbed into the group, but also that isolation or rejection will leave us totally separate and alone. At some level, therefore, we know we are dependent on others. We know it but resent it:

> All groups stimulate and at the same time frustrate the individuals composing them; for the individual is impelled to seek the satisfaction of his needs in his group and is at the same time inhibited in this aim by the primitive fears that the group arouses. (Bion, 1961, p. 188)

Resentment and frustration can lead us to behave as if we could ignore the group when it suits us or even as if group membership is some kind of aberration or temporary state—as if really we "[do] not belong to a group at all". (Ibid., p. 168) However, Bion argued that even a hermit—apparently a clear-cut example of someone living separate from any group—actually demonstrates the opposite, showing that we cannot understand human behaviour if we do not take group membership into account: "You cannot understand a recluse living in isolation unless you inform yourself about the group of which he is a member. To argue that in such a case one is not dealing with a group is merely to prove oneself naïvely imperceptive." (Ibid., p. 133) This view is supported by Thomas Merton's description of his life as a hermit where he identified his apparent separation from the group as the very definition of his connectedness to it: "my solitude is my place in society." (Cited in France, 1997, p. 182)

Every moment in every group is therefore impregnated with an awareness that is sometimes consciously present, but always unconsciously active, of this generally unrecognised dimension of experience in others and also in ourselves. Partly as a result of our groupishness we cannot control groups—and often cannot even control ourselves in groups. Cooperation in groups is always both an opportunity and a problem.

Cooperation as a political process

Bion may have created the word groupishness, but he was well aware that there is a long history to the idea that we are "political animals". Aristotle described the *polis*, the Greek city state, as "the only framework within which man can fully realize his spiritual, moral and intellectual capacities". (Kitto, 1957, p. 78) Bion attributed similar qualities to the group: "I consider that group mental life is essential to the full life of the individual", (1961, p. 54), "the human individual is a political animal and cannot find fulfilment outside a group and cannot satisfy any emotional drive without expression of its social component." (1967, p. 118)

On the other hand, however, we are also undeniably individuals in the everyday sense of the word so that the magnetic pull of the group side of our make-up can block the satisfaction of an individual's needs just as easily as it can meet them. We can experience group membership as a burden, an imposition that prevents us from doing or getting what we want at that moment. In such moments, we resent the group experience because we think we could do better on our own—or the opposite: we blame the group because we feel they have left us to do it all on our own and are out of our depth. Either way, we tend to hold individual group members or the group as a whole responsible for our dissatisfaction.

The following story illustrates this dynamic of frustration:

> A learning group comprised of students in their late twenties was in
> the fourth session of an organisation studies module on a full-time

postgraduate programme. The group of thirty-two participants had been together for only two weeks and were sitting around tables in already established groups of five or six. In this session they were working in these groups on a structured activity designed to address the topics of organisational structure and culture. One of the groups had gone to work in another room.

After forty minutes, one member of this group came back in to ask the tutor to go to see them. The tutor went in to find the group extremely unhappy: "We're spending far too long on this sort of stuff and we're not getting anything out of it. We don't understand what's going on." The tutor replied forcefully, "It sounds like you're blaming me." Immediately, two of them countered, defensively, "No, no. What we're saying is—we don't know what we're getting out of this." Another member continued, "We look at some of the other groups and they just get on with this stuff and they seem to get loads out of it. We're not getting anything and we feel stuck in this group. What we'd like is to move into some of the other groups a bit more and work with different people but we're not allowed to." One group member said, "I went in there just now and went up to a table and Kevin looked at me and said 'What do you want?'. All I wanted was to go and say 'Hi' but he just told me to 'Get lost'. That's what the group is like."

Back in the large group in the review session this small group were unable to express their strength of feeling; merely commenting, "It would be quite nice to move around a bit. We're really happy in our group."

In Bion's writing, and in the most typical ways his thinking has been taken up and developed by others, it is this negative experience of groupishness that dominates; the downside of its impact on group dynamics is emphasised to the exclusion of the upside. Bion clearly set the tone in this describing himself at one point, for example, as "suffering, as all members of the group suffer, through dislike of the emotional quality in myself and in the group that is inherent in membership of the group". (1961, p. 116) It was an important insight, emphasising just how easily this instinctive push–pull between individual and group tendencies can throw us off course. The situation is all the more volatile as a result of the fact that as the individual's inner experience of the tension is both conscious and unconscious, so this "emotional quality in myself" can all too easily translate into external relations between group members.

Despite many assertions in *Experiences in Groups* of an apparently unquestionable dislike of the experience of groupishness, nowhere does Bion suggest that it might also be possible to revel in its emotional quality in himself or others. The strength of this dominantly negative view has made it almost impossible even to see another side, that is, not merely the need for the group but the potential delight to be had in cooperative activity.

David Armstrong is one of the few writers to have given more balanced attention to both sides of the experience of groupishness, arguing that it "qualifies both work-group and basic-assumption mentality and not just the latter". (2005, p. 144) Eric Miller too has suggested that "whilst [groupishness] carries an ever-present risk of homogenization, [it] is also a necessary basis for combining in cooperation—in working together on a task". (1998, p. 51) Fear of this "ever-present risk" has led to an emphasis on the way individual difference can be swallowed up in a group assumption. Very few analyses of Bion's ideas identify, as Miller does here, what might be called the positive contribution of groupishness. It is a necessary basis for cooperation in groups and the pursuit of truth can be boosted by giving attention in the moment to the multiple levels of interaction that occur between the individual and group elements of experience.

However, his word "basis" suggests the metaphor of foundation and structure that does not fully convey the dynamic nature of the phenomena that arise from the impact of groupishness. What Bion—and here Miller—seem to have identified was not a "system", with a base and dependent superstructure, but rather a dynamic process with two opposed cycles of interaction: the one open and "virtuous", the other closed and "vicious".

In the virtuous cycle, which is characterised and fuelled by attention, group members are able to mobilise the complex reality of their shared experience of groupishness. In pursuing truth they can attend to being both an individual and a group member, to both their primary narcissism and their "social-ism". (Bion, 1967, p. 118; 1994, p. 122) The combination is potent: it can allow both individuals and the group as a whole to have a voice, to thrive on and learn from inherent differences among them, and to treat emotional experience, including conflict and disagreement, as sources of information which can enhance development (see Armstrong, 2005, pp. 90–110). Narcissism and socialism, whether in each member's individual experience or between members, are not experienced as being in conflict but rather in tension and that tension can in turn be a source of fresh thinking and creativity.

The vicious cycle, on the other hand, is characterised and fuelled by distraction, with group members turning their backs on truths that may be represented by the new, by differences between unique individuals, and by a negative experience of the tensions that groupishness arouses. In place of attention and purpose, they seek an illusory comfort or security in which a distorted sense of group identity and the need for survival come before the truth and even before the purpose for which they have met. This is the "ever-present risk of homogenization".

We would like at this point to use the example of the work of Ivan Illich to illustrate how groupishness can stimulate and support cooperation rather than undermining it. Whilst his work has always remained somewhat outside the mainstream, Illich was one of the most provocative thinkers of the twentieth century, developing with others a radical critique of many of the sacred cows of modern society, such as education, medicine, the Church, the concept of the individual, the negative impact of technology, development, communication, transportation, speed, and scale.

In his work over many decades, Illich deliberately drew on the creative energy inherent in the tension between group and individual identity. He believed in the power of the collective, and in his practice favoured what he called "conviviality". Going a step beyond "cooperation", conviviality suggests a way of life shared with others—con- + vivere, living together—not just sharing in the endeavour of work—co- + operari, working together.

> To give an example of how he worked, Illich describes an occasion where a professor commented on Illich's multilingual upbringing: "I am a psychologist but you look quite balanced for a man who has been brought up multilingual." This chance encounter led Illich to question the assumptions behind the remark. His research revealed an extensive literature on multilingualism but what struck him was that it was all based on a pervasive and apparently unquestioned assumption: that to be multilingual is the exception and that humans are by nature monolingual—in his phrase, "*Homo monolinguis est*".

> He had a hunch, however, that this assumption might simply
> be untrue, that it "might be a very recent invention related to the
> creation of nation-states." But that was it; it remained a hunch. An
> apparently simple question had led him to a deeper issue but one
> which he could take no further on his own. It was an experience
> he recognised: "So," he adds, "as I always do on these occasions,
> I called together friends to discuss this question." (Cayley, 1992,
> pp. 90–91)

From many years' experience, Illich had learned that questions of this
kind—"unasked" questions, as it were, ones that slip between the gaps
in the accepted categories of everyday understanding—can only truly
be addressed in a particular matrix. This matrix, which involves individuals thinking together in a group, amounts to the simultaneous
mobilisation of both aspects of our groupishness.

Carl Mitcham describes Illich's working principle as, "repeated,
focused conversation with a small circle of colleagues". (2002, p. 13)
Illich himself talked of such "colleagues" as friends, basing the idea
on a view of friendship that helps to understand the creative side of
groupishness. Illich was steeped in the ancient tradition of friendship
where much more is implied than the sense of personal intimacy, which
dominates the modern view. In the ancient tradition, friendship was
seen above all as the expression of a life choice: friends are engaged in
the pursuit of truth—they are *philo-sophers*, that is, "friends of wisdom
and learning". Their search for truth is both individual and cooperative;
it depends on a capacity to identify with one's individual and group
selves and on a readiness to be taken up in the group while remaining true to oneself. One of Illich's "friends" describes an experience of
encountering this principle in practice:

> Crossing over the threshold of his [Illich's] rented house that first
> time, I suffered the natural fear of one who enters uninvited the
> home of another. Still, I came, beckoned to the feast by the friend
> of a friend of Illich. Once inside, the fear of coldness and distance
> meted out to the uninvited gate-crasher vanished. Immediately,
> the sitting circle immersed in convivial contemplative conversa-
> tion silently moved and shifted to create a space that included me.
> Unasked for, a steaming cup of coffee appeared from somewhere.
> Seconds later, attentive like the others, puzzling and mulling over a

yet-to-be-grasped notion, I fully forgot that I had not been invited.
(Prakash, 2002, p. 141)

Illich's faith in convivial, contemplative, and focused conversation
among friends moved well beyond just "a small circle". It became an
organising principle for his life, a working method for cooperation,
rooted in the mobilisation of groupishness—although of course this
is Bion's term not his. The link between these elements is reflected in
Illich's description of the centre for cross-cultural studies that he established in Mexico in 1961 as "in its deepest sense a contemplative place".
(du Plessix Gray, 1970, p. 275) In the traditional language of spirituality,
contemplation is synonymous with attention.

The importance of this example is that it illustrates the potential for
groupishness to become the basis for an energised and energising, even
joyous, experience of cooperation. How exactly this occurs is mysteri-
ous but again the friendship tradition offers a clue. From its beginnings
in the ancient world *parrhesia*, or "frankness of speech"—the opposite
of flattery—was identified as a key element of true friendship. Foucault
summarised the concept and practice in a way that emphasises its
individual–group dimension:

> [*Parrhēsia* is] verbal activity in which a speaker expresses his per-
> sonal relationship to truth, and risks his life because he recognizes
> truth-telling as a duty to help improve or help other people (as
> well as himself). In *parrhēsia*, the speaker uses his freedom and
> chooses frankness instead of persuasion, truth instead of falsehood
> or silence, the risk of death instead of life and security, criticism
> instead of flattery, and moral duty instead of self-interest and moral
> apathy. (Foucault, 2001, pp. 19–20)

This frankness of speech, or "fearless speech", as Foucault called it,
involves a readiness to speak directly to the other, regardless of rank,
because it is based on the assumption that a relationship of friendship
is rooted in the search for truth. In these circumstances, Bion's notion
of the individual as a "group animal at war" may still be apt—even if
the battle is emotional and intellectual rather than physical. However,
any wounds or scars that are inflicted by a friend have the potential to
be acknowledged and attended to because they are understood to be an
unavoidable element in the process of working cooperatively together.

The potential for cooperation in groupishness

A friend of ours works in a studio run by a photographers' co-operative which she helped to set up with a group of like-minded colleagues some years ago. They had all been looking for a space to work in but also needed to share the cost of expensive, high-tech equipment and technical support, which none of them could afford as individuals. In addition, many of them had already experienced the benefits of working alongside others in what can be a lonely occupation. The co-op rents studio space from a larger organisation whose aim is to support the work of creative individuals, including artists, designers, musicians, and writers, and also to promote the development of a wide range of small, start-up businesses in this field. In addition to artists' studios the building houses an exhibition space, a film studio, meeting rooms and conference facilities, a crèche, a café-restaurant, and a bookshop.

After many years of stability, however, things are changing for the photographic co-op. Members face what is probably their biggest decision in twenty years: following lengthy negotiations they must choose whether or not to amalgamate with the larger organisation, which is trying to rationalise under one "house brand" all of the activities it supports. The dilemma for co-op members is that by becoming a part of something larger they risk losing some of the independence they now enjoy. On the other hand, if they do not join they may lose the space altogether—and possibly sooner rather than later as their current rental agreement is only guaranteed for one more year.

Suddenly nothing is certain anymore and the threat of change has evoked a strong emotional response, generating intense feelings for and against the proposed amalgamation, which is referred to by some as a "partnership"—something others refuse even to contemplate. Unexpectedly, the threat has also brought to the surface significant differences of opinion within the co-op, which until now they had seemed able to ignore.

We have known members of this co-operative for many years and they have always seemed to us to manage the competing demands of the individual and the group with creativity and imagination. If you wanted a snapshot of the pleasures and potential inherent in human groupishness then you could hardly have done better than look at this group. Each member could point to specific benefits they had gained as an individual from membership of the co-op. Some of these were social, from combating the isolation and loneliness of the work to life-long friendships; others were more obviously professional, from the development or exchange of ideas and practical tips to sharing the cost and use of equipment or collaborating over joint projects and exhibitions. When two members married, everyone cooperated to produce a joint photographic record of the occasion as if to symbolise the conviviality of their groupishness.

Now, however, the proposed amalgamation has created waves that have rocked the boat more violently than anyone would have predicted. Alongside many practical issues, group members are grappling with fundamental questions of identity, which highlight individual–group tensions that the founding members thought they had dealt with long ago. No one seems to know whether they will find or lose themselves in the proposed wider grouping, whether as individuals or as a co-operative. As one member put it, "We'd got so used to dealing with our own stuff, we forgot about the outside world ... took our eye off the ball, as it were—or kept our eye on our own ball, but forgot we were part of a bigger game."

The group seemed to have developed a fantasy about their uniqueness, which led them to ignore the possibility that their existence could ever be under threat. (Levine, 2001, p. 1253) When people started to talk about the wider, umbrella organisation as a "parent", the idea produced a strongly negative response in some but an equally positive one for others. As a whole, they appeared both to want and to resent "parental" control, a mixed reaction that may have been generated by quite stark differences of opinion, hidden until now, about their own leadership in recent years.

It has been interesting to observe how their language has become increasingly military in tone with talk at a pre-vote meeting of "taking sides", "preparing ammunition", "forming alliances", and "digging in". After an open meeting with representatives of the larger organisation, they began to talk about the approaching "battle", and of being "swallowed up" by the larger organisation. As decision day approaches individual co-op members have begun to say they must "take a stand" and "refuse to budge". A solicitor has been appointed.

However, the idea of the co-op being "swallowed up" also produced a somewhat counter-intuitive, positive response. Maybe because she uses mythical and religious imagery in her work, one woman recalled the universal theme of the hero swallowed by a "whale" as part of the journey to fulfilment. She said that mythologies worldwide represent this symbolic death as a magical threshold leading to a metamorphosis in the internal life and spiritual development of the individual that has implications for society. (Campbell, 1975, pp. 79–83) Her comments brought home to other co-op members the way their combative use of military language seemed to go against all of their co-operative ideals and did not fit with their sense of themselves as a group. It also allowed them to admit that actually they had been aware that they did not all agree about the purpose of the co-op and the way it had been developing, but the differences had never been properly aired. As one of them put it, "Things seemed to be working OK, so I couldn't see the point in stirring things up."

At the time of writing, there is no way of knowing how this situation will resolve itself but, however it turns out, it has highlighted the nature of the choices we make in relation to our groupishness. Joining or forming a group is an active choice, which requires a capacity for persistence in attention if it is to turn out well. Group membership implies a need to engage with things I am not used to because the group and individual parts of myself and others come together in the group.

In this case, co-op members have begun to recognise that in order to know who they are in relation to each other, they also have to acknowledge their relatedness to the larger organisation and to the wider artistic and business worlds in which they work. They can now see how the prospect of amalgamation created an external enemy—a "them"—onto whom they could transfer the painful reality of their internal disagreements. One member even said they could now see that there might be real benefits to be gained from cooperating with the wider grouping, fighting alongside the perceived enemy to support other creative individuals and businesses in a hostile and difficult economic, social, and artistic environment.

Unconscious communications in working groups

There is one final aspect to the already complex set of relationships invoked by cooperation in groups. It concerns the way in which the dynamics of groupishness are communicated between group members. Bion reminds us that much of what passes between people in groups is a form of unconscious communication, so that for much of the time we do not know what we are doing in groups or why we are doing it.

A client recently told us a story that illustrates how much communication can be hidden in this way. We recognised the story, because we have had similar experiences to his and have frequently observed the phenomenon in groups.

> John was one of a team of trainers leading an intensive workshop on group dynamics. On the first day, his colleagues acted in a way that made him feel put down and under attack although he could not understand why. It involved a workshop he was going to run with three other colleagues for a new client group. In a sense, this was his client: he had worked with the CEO for some years and had negotiated this new contract. He was also the most experienced member of the team, which he had created in the first place some years earlier. However, in the planning session he found that his colleagues had somehow assumed that he would do the introductions, but that they would then run the introduction proper. He did not have any doubts about their competence and had often worked with them in just this way, but at that moment he somehow felt squeezed or pushed out.
>
> He did not say anything about his experience because he could not work out what to say, and also because he could not be sure whether he was just being over-sensitive. As he left at the end of a long day he felt quite pleased at how he had dealt with the moment—not over-reacting, not making a mountain out of a molehill. However, the next morning he was late for that crucial opening session despite the fact that he was the only person who lived locally.
>
> What struck John most forcibly after this event was the complex way in which all of this had happened. He described the strength of his feelings as he fought his way through traffic jams in a desperate attempt to get to the workshop in time for the start: "I felt I was going to die!" However, the most telling point was that his late arrival (only by one or two minutes) undermined the very decision about starting that session that had caused him so much grief the previous day. He had not reacted at the time to his experience of being attacked and dismissed, and had felt pleased that he had "dealt with it" on his own—but here he was now retaliating against the others, as it were—although quite unintentionally—by undermining their decision of the previous evening.

This story points to the number of levels at which the emotional experience of our groupishness is communicated between people in groups. What had the group or individual group members put into John on the first day? What had he taken in and what had he put back into the group by keeping silent about his experience? How had this mixture of feelings contributed to his lateness the next morning? What had he communicated by being late? What had they all done to compromise their ability to cooperate?

This "putting in" and "taking out" of impressions and emotions can be rather obvious, as when one person is asked to leave a group or another is welcomed in. However, Bion's insight was to recognise that whatever explicit messages there may be, there is always an unconscious dimension to such communications (1961, p. 116) and that this is as true of attention as it is of distraction: work-group mentality "exerts an influence on our experience in groups that can be no less unconscious than the basic assumptions". (Armstrong, 2005, p. 146) As a result, the complexity of group experience in the moment can never be mapped. Because they are made "anonymously", (Bion, 1961, p. 54) the contributions that individuals make are likely to remain unrecognised either by the group or by the individuals themselves. This is true of our acts of cooperation as well as of the times when, as group animals at war, we seek to sabotage or otherwise distract the group from its common purpose.

CHAPTER FIVE

Purpose

Purpose is of central importance in groups because of the fact that people always meet with something in mind. "Every group, however casual, meets to 'do' something", as Bion puts it with typical directness and simplicity. (1961, p. 143) He argues that this is why a defining characteristic of groups that function well is their sense of "common purpose": (1961, p. 25) what they are there to do is agreed, understood, and shared by all. This understanding of purpose is a good starting point for making sense of one's experience in groups, because so often the purpose for which a group is meeting is not clearly stated, or even when it is, can easily be forgotten. Bion used his experience of the group purpose as the basis for spotting moments when it turned into something different—typically without discussion or even apparent awareness.

Our primary focus in this chapter, therefore, is to bring to attention "the beauty of common purpose"; (Cocker, 2007, p. 136) that is, its role, importance, and implications for practice in groups.

However, we will also question a simplistic notion of purpose. Achieving clarity over a common purpose can be far from straightforward, and in this instance Bion's directness and simplicity are not entirely helpful. There is a danger of being lulled by a naïve understanding of purpose into a false sense that we know what to focus upon or what the answer should be. In *Experiences in Groups*, Bion gives little attention to the possibility that determining a common purpose might in itself be contentious, other than in highlighting the potentially negative reaction of group members to a leader. This might have arisen in part from the fact that his ideas were strongly influenced by the military settings of his first experiments. In such a context, it was widely understood at the time that the formal leader had the authority, indeed the responsibility, to establish a common aim. Once this is established, the primary challenge for the leader can be to withstand hostility from the group and its members when they do not wish to keep to this purpose.

In many settings, the simple notion of establishing and maintaining a sense of common purpose through the authority of the leader is just not adequate. Our experience in most modern (non-military) organisations is that there is a greater requirement for the whole group to be involved in establishing and maintaining the sense of purpose. Individuals and groups are frequently not prepared to meekly accept a purpose given from above, and institutional rules and procedures often do not support leaders in imposing top-down directives.

In this chapter, we will begin with what is likely to be the most valuable idea for the majority of groups: getting in touch with their purpose. This idea will then be further refined by looking at the process of clarifying purpose and the challenges that this poses. In the final section, we will return to a consideration of the challenge of cooperation, looking in particular at the way groupishness plays out in the relationship between group purpose and individual purposes. The need to focus attention on these issues is an important one because of the inherent instability of group life that Bion identified so strongly.

Getting in touch with the group's purpose

Purpose has the potential to structure and support group life rather in the way the central pole supports a tent. Attention to purpose can therefore act as a touchstone to evaluate whether or not the activity of the group is on track.

The issue can be expressed in the question: what is the difference between a group that works to achieve its purpose and one that does not? It is our experience that individuals in groups typically treat this as simple and straightforward. Too frequently group members do not know what it is they are there to do: they may have forgotten it, simply never have been told, or it may be kept secret, avoided, and lied about, or otherwise corrupted. Importantly, absence of attention to purpose does not lead to inactivity. Instead, another purpose tends to emerge that may not have been discussed; group members might not even be able to tell you what it is but it is evident from their behaviours that there is one.

To emphasise the importance of purpose in this way is not new. For instance, Vaill suggests, "the definition and clarification of purposes is both a fundamental step in effective strategic management and a prominent feature of every high-performing system I have ever investigated." (Vaill, 1998, p. 37) Purpose goes by many names: aim, core business, vision, mission, strategy, task, primary task, primary spirit, guiding spirit, intention, *raison d'être*, "knitting" (as in, "stick to the knitting"), and "talk" (as in, "walk the talk"). It can also involve different levels, rather in the way attention can be focused or free-floating:

> A sense of purpose is not the same as a clearly defined purpose. A sense of purpose generates defined purposes within any given context ... Defined purposes are the single most important source of orientation in doing both technical and adaptive work, like a ship's compass heading at sea. But even more precious than any defined purpose is a sense of purpose that can enable one to step back and review, perhaps with doubt, perhaps with delight, the orienting values embedded in any particular mission. (Heifetz, 1994, p. 274)

Whilst these may be familiar ideas, Bion recognised the powerful unconscious dynamics that undermine a purely rational approach to defining purpose. He had a remarkable ability to notice the tendency for groups—typically without even realising it—to lose touch with the agreed purpose and unconsciously replace it with a pseudo—or "as-if" purpose. The result can be an impression of progress towards an agreed end whilst in fact the group is working in an altogether different direction.

We begin with a story where this is the main theme. It concerns a group that lost touch with its purpose but was able to return to it through the intervention of one group member who instinctively understood the importance of keeping the common purpose clearly in mind. Things were getting out of hand because the purpose had been forgotten, but her awareness and intervention had a transformative impact. The meeting involved a community group in a small Scottish town and was initiated by the flyer reproduced below. It had been circulated to local residents inviting them to discuss a proposal for lighting in the local BMX Park. One of those attending was Fiona, the person we happened to be staying with. Because it would eat into our time together she nearly decided not to go—in which case events at the meeting might have taken a very different turn.

LIGHTING IN THE BMX PARK

Meeting at Hockey Club, 7 p.m. Friday 26th July

You are invited to come with your neighbours to a meeting about lighting in the BMX park. It will take place at the *Hockey Club at 7 p.m. on Friday 26th July*. The meeting will be chaired by Councillor Dr. Rupert McBride and hosted by the Community Development Trust, which is providing funding for the lighting.

The purpose of the meeting is to hear the views of interested stakeholders on lighting for the BMX park. Stakeholders include: neighbours, the Police, a representative of the businesses on the industrial estate, a youth worker, BMX park users, parents and local councillors. The lighting is to be operated on a timer, and one of the objectives of the meeting is to decide on times for the lighting to be switched on and off. There will be a live demonstration of the lighting by the installers, so everyone can see exactly what is being proposed.

Other things to discuss include the setting up of a Monitoring Committee to include park users.

This flyer brought two dozen local people to the Hockey Club under the experienced chairmanship of Councillor Dr. Rupert McBride, a well-known figure in the community. At the end of the meeting, the proposal to introduce lighting in the BMX Park was supported unanimously. However, for most of the meeting it did not seem likely that such a positive outcome would be reached.

The tone of the meeting was set right from the start with the airing of strongly held, differing opinions. One stakeholder group—three or four vocal "neighbours" who lived on the edge of the park—did indeed take the opportunity to express their views to the officials who had turned up to hear them—the Police, the representative from the industrial estate, the youth worker, and local councillors.

The heated and fast-moving discussion quickly raised a wide range of contentious issues:

- the misuse of drugs and alcohol by young people in the park
- rubbish and litter, especially broken glass
- noise from the "kids"—especially at night, sometimes till 2 or 3 a.m.
- the fact that bins were not being cleared when they should be.

The last issue was particularly fresh in their minds: this meeting was taking place on a Friday, which happened to be the official bin-clearance day but that day they had not been emptied. The argument was forcibly made that because council tax payers' money was involved, the Town Council should be telling the District Council responsible for emptying the bins, how and when this should be done, not the other way round. At some point during the meeting, the neighbours "had a go" at all three councillors present.

Cllr McBride attempted to counter these attacks and gave an example of another frequently raised complaint, which concerned cars driving at 50 m.p.h. up the local high street. It was intended as an example of the gap between people's perceptions of things and the reality that very few cars, if any, do travel at such speeds. However, the example proved to be more of a distraction than a help, as "reckless", "inconsiderate" driving was another contentious issue in the town; like noise in the park it was often associated with young people. Far from settling the tensions, this intervention from the chair actually fanned the flames beneath the already overheated pressure cooker of the meeting.

Eventually Fiona spoke up, making two points. First, she said that all of the opinions being voiced were "right"—in the sense that each person's perspective, whether personal or official, was based on their own experience. However much they argued, everyone could surely accept that the views expressed were all true from the speaker's perspective at least. This open acknowledgment and affirmation of people's very differing opinions seemed to damp down the anger for a moment—long enough for her second comment to build on the calming effect of the first. She simply pointed out that although all of the issues that had been aired were real and important, they actually had nothing to do with the purpose of the meeting, which was just about lighting. This intervention allowed other people to find their voice, such as another local resident, a passionate supporter of young people, who believed that there was a chronic lack of facilities for youth in the town. Both the tone and content of the discussion shifted, allowing the chair to keep the rest of the meeting focused on the purpose, with the related proposals ultimately receiving unanimous support.

All too often we assume that working in groups is a purely rational affair, but the reason individuals and groups are prepared to put their efforts into achieving a purpose is that the outcome means something to them—it matters. Meaning is emotional as well as rational: it is about caring. In this story, we see emotions driving the agenda right from the beginning, a phenomenon that is so common that it is surprising only in the fact that it so often comes as a surprise to those involved. The initial clash of emotions, which only increased as time passed, fuelled the distractions and threatened to prevent any of the meeting's objectives from being properly addressed, let alone achieved. It took an intervention at a crucial moment by our friend to return the meeting to its purpose.

So what actually happened? After all, the fact that the final agreement was unanimous indicates that the proposal for lighting may not in itself have been all that controversial. The trigger seems to have been a specific phrase from the flyer—"to hear the views of ... neighbours ..."—which took on a life of its own and allowed the meeting, without anyone realising it, to move in an unintended direction. The actual purpose of the meeting—"to hear ... views ... on lighting for the BMX park"—shifted, apparently unnoticed, and certainly unchallenged, to a new one.

Initiated by the neighbours' agenda, the meeting seemed to have been turned into an opportunity for local people to have their views and grievances heard on any matter of relevance to the council and other authority figures present in the room. None of these grievances appeared to have anything at all to do with the issue of lighting. Even the two-to-three-in-the-morning noise issue was not relevant as the proposal only suggested lighting the BMX Park up to 9.00 or 9.30 p.m. The lighting issue disappeared under the mass of other complaints that had been waiting in the wings for a chance to have their moment in the limelight. The speed of the change can probably be traced to the two key elements of the purpose: first, as we have suggested, the phrase "to hear views" evoked views on all kinds of local issues; second, the make-up of the group brought together an unusually rich mix, representing a wide range of differing and conflicting interests: local residents, BMX park users, local officials, and the police.

Of course, any meeting can turn out like this but not all do. In the end, this one returned very effectively to the task in hand. At one point, Bion writes that "organization and structure" are key "weapons" in a group's armoury, (1961, p. 170) enabling it to carve out the mental space necessary for remaining attentive to their purpose. He might perhaps have said "tools" or "means" but somehow "weapons" does reflect the force, determination, and skill that are sometimes required for a group to fight its way back to an awareness of purpose.

In this case, the main organisational structure, both practically and symbolically, was the role of chair held by Dr. McBride. As an experienced councillor and meeting chairman, he might have been expected simply to acknowledge the range of complaints being made in order then to remind everyone that they were here "to hear the views ... on lighting for the BMX park". However, the pressure of the moment led him to come out of role. Rather than sticking with his own task, which was to manage the discussion and keep everyone on track, he allowed himself to become involved in the actual argument. In the face of what he clearly experienced as attacks he felt the need to defend.

This is a good example of how the power and speed of unfolding group dynamics can take off-guard even the most capable of people. Bion is clear that many of these dynamics are unconscious, so that it is not uncommon in the moment to be absolutely convinced that the group purpose is being pursued—and only later to wonder how it was possible to have become so side-tracked.

In this instance, what brought the group back to its intended purpose was an intervention made by one participant who managed in the midst of the escalating argument to keep her attention on the actual purpose of the meeting. It is not easy to say why Fiona was able to keep her head clear, but it might have been because she was less emotionally involved and did not go the meeting with a strong personal agenda—in fact, nearly did not go at all and was keen to get back home. In general, a degree of stoic indifference—engaged care, but with a strong attachment to the outcome—can help to keep attention on the group purpose.

The power of Fiona's intervention was reflected in the fact that at the end of the meeting people from each of the extremes in the argument approached her to thank her and even ask her to become involved in other issues. It was as if she had directly addressed, and thereby some-how contained and settled, the emotions that had led the group to become distracted from its intended purpose in the first place. Young and old felt that she had understood their perspective.

There is one element missing from this story, which we only became aware of when we sent it to Fiona to be sure she was happy for us to use it here. What she told us gave us a fresh insight into her state of mind during the meeting, revealing just what it took for her to inter-vene as she did. It turns out that she was in a state of greatly heightened anxiety—to the point where she found herself on the brink of tears. One difficulty was that she knew all the people who had diverted the discussion away from the lighting proposal—that is, from the purpose of the meeting—and who were now arguing about other things, espe-cially the behaviour of young people, and acting almost as if they had come to make trouble. One of them in particular, a very strong character who was taking the lead, was her next-door neighbour. Fiona really did not know what would happen if she spoke up, aware that he might take it as a personal attack. So her feelings were mixed: she was now deeply engaged in the topic and also keen to move things on so that she could return home, but also frightened or at least seriously con-cerned about how this neighbour might react and about possible future repercussions.

When she told us all of this, we realised we could just as well have used her story to illustrate the experience of groupishness because her emotions in the moment reflected so vividly the tension between her anxieties as an individual and her sense of commitment to the group. In the end it seems she managed to steer a path between the two by acknowledging the validity of each individual's point of view, but then reminding everyone of the group purpose. Somehow this changed things.

Fiona's story illustrates the way strongly felt emotion can distract a group from its purpose, but also the power of attention—evenly sus-pended and focused—to bring people back to their senses and to a col-lective sense of purpose. Attention in the moment, the search for truth, a keen awareness of purpose, and the creative potential of groupishness—all of these elements can be seen to have played their part.

The challenge of clarifying purpose

It is probably not an exaggeration to say that the events in this story are illustrative of the rule rather than the exception: the experience of working in groups is frequently affected by insufficient clarity of purpose. This is understandable because, like the pursuit of truth, a moment by moment clarity of purpose is probably best thought of as an aspiration rather than as an achievable objective. However, our assumption is that working to achieve clarity is always valuable, if not always enjoyable, because it will produce an expression of truth however partial, and the disclosure of truth is always transformative.

Lack of clarity in relation to purpose often arises from negligence or ignorance but sometimes it is deliberate. The following brief story involves a senior manager who worked from the assumption that seeking to achieve clarity of purpose would cause more problems than it was worth because it was likely to distract staff from what he needed them to do. This sort of management logic reminded Robert of working in a school where the head teacher only ever organised meetings with small sub-groups of staff because, he said, "When all the staff are together the meeting just turns into a criticism of me"! He was not entirely wrong—but whilst this head teacher may have benefitted in one way from hearing less criticism, there was also a cost because he limited his exposure to the truth of what his staff members thought and felt. In the same way, there is a cost when managers assume that seeking clarity of purpose is detrimental to the work.

> After three months the company re-organisation had reached a critical stage. The steering group had determined the key parameters for change and it had been decided that there would be five departments—a reduction of one. They had discussed the potential for radical change at the regular, and sometimes lengthy, planning meetings. However, at recent meetings a recurring theme had been the possibility that there would actually be very little change.
>
> Nathan, senior manager and chair of the steering group, had done an MBA and he knew that it was important to get people's commitment in a change process by involving them in the planning process. This process, which so far had involved just the steering

group, had taken longer than anticipated and was already behind schedule, so he decided that now was the time to draw others in to contribute.

Two members of the steering group were given the job of drafting a message inviting staff members to the first workshop, which would focus on the task of producing proposals for how the five departments would be set up. The draft message was given to Nathan to sign off before being circulated and he was happy with all of it, apart from the first paragraph:

> "The purpose of restructuring the departments is to stream-line our processes and refocus the organisation to be more customer-facing."

He made some minor amendments to wording throughout the document but deleted the whole of the statement of purpose. He explained, without inviting discussion, "I want them to get on with the job of redesign—I do not want the workshop hijacked by a debate about purpose. We'll end up in a row about whether this is all about downsizing and efficiency gains." He was well aware of the tone of the corridor conversations that were taking place and the increasing nervousness amongst staff about possible redundancies. He explained, "I don't want to let the reorganisa-tion drag on any longer than it had to" and told them to email the message out to staff without the statement of purpose.

Of course Nathan was correct that opening up a discussion of pur-pose raised the possibility that the meeting would not achieve what he wanted it to, so his action could be interpreted as a perceptive interven-tion by an experienced manager. We do not question the fact that work-ing to achieve clarity of purpose can be a difficult thing to do. However, this story also suggests one of the reasons why such clarity is impor-tant: without it there is likely to be an increasing passivity within the group, a tendency to settle for the status quo. This is not because peo-ple assume that the purpose is staying the same, but because they do not know what the purpose is in the first place. The consequent lack of direction leads to a lack of creative energy in the group—the very oppo-site of the stated intention to involve people in the planning process in order to increase buy-in to the changes. There is some evidence in this case that there was ambiguity, even within the steering group, about the purpose of the reorganisation, and this manifested in an increasing sense that nothing would really change.

The tension between individual and group purposes

When a manager seeks to achieve his or her purpose by manipulating the group it is an example of the inappropriate use of power: politics in a negative sense. The intention is understandable, however. In the example above, the manager sought to manage the tension between individual interests and his perception of collective, group interests. He did not want the workshop "hijacked" by a discussion of the broad purpose because he believed there was a more important job to do. His approach, therefore, was to play down or deny the tension between possibly conflicting interests or purposes. Of course this is a managerial fantasy because the tension exists and it does not simply go away if it is ignored.

This experience reflects the conflicted emotions set up by the experience of our groupishness that continually threaten to undermine group cooperation. To take groupishness seriously in this context requires giving attention to the contradictory motivations that are present rather than turning a blind eye to them. On the one hand, the pull is to cooperate in pursuit of a common group purpose potentially at the expense of individual aspirations; on the other, there is a motivation to act as "a group animal at war" pursuing individual purposes with vigour potentially at the expense of the group.

If the tension is denied or avoided, the consequence is likely to be the loss of the creativity the tension can stimulate. In this instance, this was reflected in the failure to realise the original radical ambition for the scheme and in a growing sense that there would in fact be little change of any significance. This group had become stuck because the truth of the situation was that no one was being allowed or encouraged to express genuine differences in interest, aspiration, or sense of purpose.

Even apparently simple, everyday decisions—such as whether or not to attend a meeting—can illustrate the strength and impact of the tensions between individual and group purposes. The following story shows how an explicit consideration of purpose can help draw attention to the deeper questions that arise from groupishness, as well as practical questions relating to attendance at meetings.

> Clarissa and Jeremy are members of a team of twenty specialists in their organisation. This group meets regularly, if not frequently. Both are "good citizens"—responsible, intelligent, and committed members of the group—and yet one has decided to attend all group meetings, the other to attend none.
>
> Clarissa is the team leader and as a direct consequence of taking up such a role has a strongly internalised sense of group—to the point where not attending probably does not even seem like an option. It is likely that she does not actually think she is choosing to attend although of course she would concede that a choice is always involved.
>
> Jeremy is at a very different stage of his career. He is trying to build his own reputation in several areas while at the same time having to fulfil all the regular, humdrum commitments that take so much time and energy in any job. He has decided that his own individual needs must be given priority over any possible contribution he might make at group meetings. He can also argue with some justification that by enhancing his own reputation he will at the same time help to build the reputation of the wider group.

It may sound simple to say that purpose is a central idea one can simply refer back to at moments of difficulty, but in practice the situation is far more complex. This brief example shows how just two individuals in a group came to interpret the importance of meetings very differently from the perspective of their roles. For the team leader the purpose of the group overlapped so neatly with her sense of her own role that there was simply no question of *not* attending. Jeremy also had a strong sense of purpose but in interpreting the group purpose against his individual aspirations he reached exactly the opposite conclusion to the team leader: he could not, or could no longer, see the relevance of group meetings to his work.

When we talked to these two individuals and to some of their colleagues it quickly became clear that an important contributory issue was that in fact no agreed statement of the group purpose existed. Everyone had a kind of idea of what it was but there were also stark differences depending on who we were talking to: senior management or the team leader, longer-serving group members or those who had only recently joined, organisational members in parallel groups, which might have been expected to share a very similar purpose, and external clients who used their services.

Two things seemed to be in play. The first was indeed the purpose itself—how it was defined (or not) and by whom. The second was the impact of groupishness. This was clear in the tensions between finding a shared agreement among group members on their purpose, aims, and tasks, on the one hand, and then the very obvious way individuals constantly defined and interpreted the group purpose according to their own perceived needs—or denied and ignored it altogether.

However, during these general discussions we came by chance across another group that also had a new leader-manager—new both to the role and to the organisation as a whole but with a lot of experience of similar work situations and groups.

> As a part of her effort to settle in, Miranda dedicated a great deal of time and energy to finding out whether what she thought the work was about actually fitted with what others expected and were doing. She started by reading all she could. The more she read, the more she realised how partial or unspecific all the written descriptions and definitions of the group purpose were. She became vividly aware that she would only be able to take up her role effectively if she could reach agreement with her colleagues at all levels over a shared definition of purpose. Without this, she sensed that she would always run the danger of getting caught up in apparently meaningful conversations that actually led nowhere because she would always be talking at "cross-purposes".
>
> She began to think that the lack of clarity was responsible for the fact that, from the start, she and others had come away from meetings with a very different understanding of what had been agreed—not because she had been ignored but because those present had simply heard things differently as a result of having a different purpose in mind. Eventually she realised that reaching an agreement over purpose just did not seem to be possible. Her first response was to mobilise her considerable political skills in an attempt to make things happen that matched her own understanding. However, she soon decided that under these conditions she could never be effective and so resigned.

This example of the resignation of an experienced and skilled manager demonstrates that understanding the reasons behind a group's underlying dynamics does not always lead to a resolution of the difficulties. The clarification of a common purpose, and the collective will to work together to achieve that purpose, is a political and emotional process as much as it is a rational endeavour. In this case, Miranda just did not have sufficient power and influence to achieve the cultural change required to bring clarity to the group purpose and thereby to her role. Just as the manager in the earlier example did not want purpose to be discussed at his workshop, some organisations become entrenched in intransigent political dynamics in which the powerful believe that their interests are best served by a lack of clarity. The complexity of such environments can be maddening because apparent agreement at one moment can unexpectedly morph into confusion and misunderstanding the next.

Our approach to working in groups, based on giving attention to truth, cooperation, purpose, and (as we discuss in the following chapter) forms of interaction in groups, is one way of engaging with these complex dynamics. Such an approach is an antidote to the impossible expectation of having a store of answers to the questions that arise on a moment by moment basis. Bion worked in this way in situations of uncertainty when faced with the challenge of holding irresolvable tensions, including the inherent conflict embodied in the experience of groupishness.

In relation to the impact of groupishness on purpose, two questions require attention: what do I, as an individual, want?—that is, what is my guiding purpose in what I do?; and what do we, as a group, want?—that is, what is our guiding purpose in what we are doing together?

What do I want? This question can be extremely difficult to answer satisfactorily. Frequently I just do not know what to choose from the range of possibilities available. At other times I discover that what I thought I wanted is not what I want at all. However, working in groups will be problematic unless there is some clarity over individual purpose and a commitment to taking it seriously. The consequences of a lack of clarity can be that the individual is dominated by the demands imposed by the group purpose. Alternatively, the individual may retreat from the group because the lack of a clear purpose means it is not possible for him or her to find anything of value in the group's activities and achievements.

This was not the situation for the two colleagues, one of whom chose to attend all meetings whilst the other attended none. Both in their different ways did have a clear sense of individual purpose. In particular, the team leader's individual sense of purpose was closely associated with her recent promotion to the role. Until this point she said she had frequently been a disruptive member at group meetings but the promotion had shifted power relations significantly: as an individual she was able to influence the group's purpose and activities; equally, the group could expect from her a positive contribution in support of their individual and group aspirations.

We are describing here a political process in which the outcomes emerge from a complex array of negotiations for each individual member in relation to the overall group. A wide range of questions is involved. For example: What happens if the group purpose conflicts with my individual purpose? How do I decide whether to join, or remain in, the group? What do I do if other individuals seem to be getting more from the group than I am? What happens if I am conflicted in achieving my purposes; that is, the group gives me part of what I want yet stops me from getting another part? Individual group members are more likely to be in a position to engage with these questions effectively if they have a clear sense of what they, as individuals, want. Questions of this kind are an expression of the pursuit of truth, which is likely to be of benefit to the group as well as the individual.

What do we, as a group, want? We also need to look at this negotiation from the perspective of the group, which implies, for example, addressing questions such as: How should the collective, that is, the group, behave when individual purposes conflict with the common purpose? When should individuals be welcomed into the group and when refused entry or ejected? What levels of individual reward and recognition should be made by the group and how significant are issues of equity?

In this way, the group–individual tension that Bion describes as groupishness is reflected in the different interpretations of purpose which exist in any group. These differences may exist not only between individuals within the group but also between the group and outsiders, some of whom may have the power to define the purpose in the first place and so to tell the group what to do. One implication of our groupishness is that we are constantly faced with the requirement to manage this negotiation between our own purposes and the common purpose of the group.

CHAPTER SIX

Forms of interaction

We turn now to the final piece in the jigsaw of Bion's ideas on groups—although as the best-known of his contributions to group theory it is often the first or only piece many people pick up. He noticed that three "patterns of behaviour" (1961, p. 175) kept appearing in group interactions: dependency, fight–flight, and pairing. He also realised that these forms of interaction can indicate a shared group mentality rather than an individual one as, for example, when a group comes to think in a dependent way and to behave accordingly. Consequently, by giving attention to the manifest behaviours within a group, we can gain an insight into the dynamics at play. Focusing on the nature and impact of the interactions can help us to understand what is going on and so provide a basis for helping the group to stay with or return to its purpose.

In this chapter, we describe the general characteristics of each form of interaction largely by means of illustration, and we explore how they can manifest in, and impact upon, group dynamics. We also focus on the ways in which they appear in groups dominated by attention as opposed to those dominated by distraction. The key question for working in groups is always the same: how can an understanding of these dynamics help to assess whether a specific interaction is being mobilised *in support of*, or *in place of*, the cooperative work of the group?

Before looking at our first illustration we offer a brief description of each of the three forms of interaction.

Dependency can be seen in the relationship—real, imagined, or hoped for—between a single leader and a follower or group of followers. It is an expression of the desire for leadership reflected in a group's relationship to an actual or fantasy leader figure and to authority in general—although Bion also suggested that all three forms of interaction "include the existence of a leader". (1961, p. 155) It is no great surprise that dependency is a central experience in human relations in groups because our dependence on others in infancy and early childhood is greater than in any other species. However, the focus of dependency in a group need not be a person at all; it is not the object of dependency that matters but rather the nature of the state of mind; that is, whether it is the expression of attention or distraction. Although dependency is, of course, often expressed through an actual relationship with a person— who can at times become a kind of group "Messiah" (ibid., p. 152)—it is equally possible for a group to look to an idea or a belief system, a longed-for "Utopia" (ibid.) or a not-to-be-questioned "bible" (ibid., p. 155), that is, a book of "rules" or set procedures based on the group's history: "That's how we've always done it!" As we have suggested, such states of mind can reflect either attention or distraction. They manifest as attention in situations that merit clear leadership and followership— most obviously, for example, in a crisis when obeying the instructions of an authoritative figure or following designated rules for evacuation. At a less extreme level, the acknowledgement of a manager's decision-making authority can be one basis for the orderly, purposeful behaviour of a group of staff. As distraction, dependency can be evident in unthinking behaviour on the part of group members. Again, an extreme example would be the mass suicide of cult members on the instructions of the cult leader. More commonplace are examples of the passivity of group members who continue to wait to be given directions, even when it is clear what needs to be done.

Fight–flight can be seen in the way we stand up to or run from people and situations that we experience as challenging or threatening. Fight and flight tend to dominate group interactions in response to perceived antagonism, competition, disagreements, or threats, all of which may be real or imagined and may be seen as located within or external to the group. Because fight, flight, and "freeze" are built into the human psyche, it is inevitable that they are present in any human grouping. As in all animals, albeit in different ways, they represent primary survival responses in the face of danger, anxiety, hate, anger, or aggression. The freeze response may be thought of as a sub-set of flight rather than as a separate phenomenon: fleeing by staying motionless as a way to avoid detection. Fight and flight can manifest as attention when different members of the group acknowledge that they hold different perceptions of a situation and are prepared to address the real challenge to group effectiveness such differences can represent. For example, newly formed groups necessarily go through a phase of "storming", that is, of disagreement and conflict. This can be an important part of the learning process, as different group members come to understand not only the purpose of the group and their potential to contribute, but also gain greater knowledge of the other group members with whom they are required to cooperate. As distraction, fight and flight behaviours simply confront the perceived threats or challenges head-on; they do not address or work with them in a manner that leads to learning or development. As a result, fight and/or flight behaviours often come to be understood as "what we need to do to survive" and so become an end in themselves, replacing the actual group purpose.

Pairing can be seen in the way we link up with others in the hope of mutual support or regeneration. It describes the tendency for a couple to emerge in and from group life and then, in turn, to influence the way group members work together. Bion saw the pair as embodying an "air of hopeful expectation"; (ibid., p. 151) that is, the belief that the group does indeed have a future, however bad things may seem to be. He believed that the basis for this sense of hope and expectation was a feeling within the group that the pair can inspire the production of a "something"—a saving idea or action, or indeed a person—that will help them to move beyond their current impasse or difficulties, thereby saving them from conflicts and tensions that they experience as in some way unmanageable. Friendship is a form of pairing that can represent hopeful expectation in just this way. It has the capacity to contain anxieties and uncertainties in a way that can be generative and highly productive. The number and range of organisations, large and small, profit-making and charitable, that are born from friendship is illustrative of its creative potential. They include such well-known names as Marks and Spencer, Hewlett Packard, Aardman Animations, and Innocent Drinks. When manifesting as attention, a pair of friends can hold the tensions in the group in a way which helps them over a difficult moment. However in distraction, the emergence of a pairing can allow other group members to think they can avoid doing the emotional or practical work necessary for dealing with perceived difficulties here and now. Their hope in the pair means they feel they can just sit passively waiting for salvation to come!

These three patterns of interaction reflect both the tensions and possibilities inherent in the lives we lead together; they are necessary and natural manifestations of human relatedness that are basic to our survival and development. Bion emphasised that, in potential at least, all three forms of interaction are present in every group all of the time. If we could read the signs well enough we would surely pick up traces of each of them at any given moment. So although one form on its own can, over a long period, dominate group interactions and relationships, internal and external, groups can also shift quite rapidly from one to another.

Focusing attention on group interactions

We tell the following story to illustrate the forms of interaction in a less abstract way. It shows how focusing attention on these patterns can offer opportunities to increase cooperation and to work towards the group purpose. The story involves an early morning lecture for first-year undergraduates on a business studies programme. We tell it in the first person in order to remain true to the way it was told to us by the tutor teaching the group.

> It was the biggest lecture theatre in the university—but as I waited to begin less than eighty students appeared out of the 350 or so time-tabled to attend. The others seemed to have voted with their feet. It all felt very flat and the room seemed empty. It was 9.00 in the morning too, and everyone seemed to be only half awake. Also there was no real "group" feel at all because everyone was spread randomly around the room, individually or in small clusters, and with big, empty spaces between them.
>
> Occasionally, there was quiet conversation among friends but the general lack of responsiveness reinforced the empty feeling; they seemed present in body but not spirit. I was even aware of something

similar in myself too: I felt bored and I could not think clearly. After a few minutes I felt I was just talking rather loudly to myself. I enjoy lecturing—and I'm quite good at it—but this was like wading through tar. I wished I could be anywhere else but there.

However, my sense of professionalism and care was sufficiently intact for me to know that I could not ignore the lack of energy in the room: just boring on was not an option. I felt a responsibility to do something to try to make this a worthwhile learning experience for these students who had bothered to turn up. I know lots of things can be done to raise the energy levels and engage a group— a change in delivery style, a challenge, a different activity or form of communication, and so on.

My intuition, or experience, led me to ask a couple of direct questions to try to get some active participation. But my efforts had no obvious impact. Everyone avoided my gaze. The atmosphere still felt dead until, quite unexpectedly, a hand went up. A young man sitting almost directly in front of me answered my second question with one of his own. There was something refreshing about his youthful energy and enthusiasm but it was also startling because his question was intellectually unusual. He reframed what I'd been saying about a relatively common management issue in terms of Christian theology.

I was brought to my senses with a jolt and the rest of the group appeared to wake up too. Although taken off guard I responded as best I could in the moment—and it seemed to be good enough because he immediately offered a further Biblical analogy. The atmosphere in the room appeared to have changed completely: everyone was suddenly watching and listening, intent and interested.

I replied to his second point feeling on slightly firmer ground now. But by the time he spoke for a third time and I began to respond, I could feel the energy in the room draining away again. My attempt to engage the group had been transitory at best—and in fact only two people (one student and me) had made an active contribution during this interaction. The rest of the group had been energised briefly to listen to the question-and-answer but not enough actually to join in. After this brief hiatus the group returned to its previous unresponsive state.

The lecturer's professional experience and intuition led her to attempt to change the dominant form of interaction within the group. Although it was not ultimately successful, we would agree, based on similar teaching experience, that this was a good thing to try in this situation. However, we are increasingly inclined to draw not merely upon experience and intuition but also on Bion's insights. To do this we have learned to ask two basic questions, both of which focus on identifying the prevailing form of interaction:

1. What patterns of interaction are manifesting in the group: dependency, fight–flight, and/or pairing?
2. Do these manifest interactions suggest that the group is giving attention to the truth and reality of the situation or do they suggest a group characterised by distraction?

In relation to our illustration there can be little argument over the answer to the second question: this was a group dominated by distraction. Although the tutor did not explicitly articulate the group purpose, it must clearly have involved learning. There could be some debate about whether this learning was of an instrumental kind ("I turn up to find out what I need to pass the assessment") or concerned with genuine development (e.g., preparing students for the workplace). Whatever the precise definition, there is little actual evidence in this story to indicate much attention to learning.

Our answer to the first question will require more careful exploration, however, and we will use it to describe more clearly the nature of the different forms of interaction. We suspect that many people—including experienced educators—might quickly conclude that the class's distracted state is being expressed in the form of dependency: "The students have turned up but are expecting the tutor to do everything." This view need not have negative connotations; it could reflect the perfectly reasonable assumption that in a teaching and learning environment dependency can have a part to play. There is often an inherent inequality in both knowledge and power in the relationship between tutor and student, which is characteristic of typical leader–follower interactions. Furthermore, some individuals in the room are likely to be predisposed to a dependent relationship with the tutor. In all likelihood, there were students in the room who were in a state of attentive dependency upon the tutor: genuinely listening to what she had to say—indeed she said she had noticed a few students taking notes.

However, the fact that some individual students were purposeful and attentive—they understood the purpose of the session and were working towards it—does not change our view that the 350-strong group was collectively in a distracted state. The tension between these two positions graphically reflects the impact of groupishness on group cooperation; that is, the tension between the purposes of the individual and those of the group. So individuals in the group may well have been in a state of attention but we are seeking to identify the state of mind and form of interaction dominating the group as a whole. In this case, as we have argued, there seems little doubt about the group's distracted state. However, to assess whether it is right to see dependency as the dominant form of interaction we need now to return to the specifics of the story.

What evidence do we have of a dominant form of interaction in this group? We would suggest attention should be given to three manifestations of interaction:

- the non-attendance of over three-quarters of the group
- the tutor's description of the atmosphere: "very flat and the room seemed empty"
- the tutor's awareness of similar feelings in herself—she felt bored and did not want to be there.

If the group had indeed been dominated by dependency then it is likely that the tutor would have had a rather different sense of her impact; she might well have experienced feelings of power and control, even grandiosity, for example. In such a situation a teacher can still be capable of putting on a performance that pushes through the resistance in the followers; in a sense, he or she may be able to carry on regardless. Whilst it is unlikely that this will lead to a significant level of learning it can at least create the appearance of an active learning group. This was not the case here, however.

The evidence at the group level suggests that the dominant form of interaction was not dependency but flight. The physical dispersal of the students—around the room and the city—seemed graphically to embody the sense of a group in flight. Most telling perhaps, given that we have privileged access to her thoughts and feelings, was the tutor's own experience. She knew just how enthusiastic she was for the subject, for the specific topic that day, and for teaching in general, and she typically received good ratings in student feedback. And yet on this day, in this group, she found herself unable to think clearly. She recognised that she too was in the grip of the group mentality—to the point where all her enthusiasm, skill, and experience were not enough and she just wanted to escape: "I wished I could be anywhere else but there ..."

Although in this case flight was the expression of distraction, this is not the inevitable outcome. Flight can also be a productive form of group interaction—for example, when conflict threatens completely to derail the work. Could this situation be a case in point? The purpose was learning and learning depends on the interplay of ideas, perspectives, people, and experiences—all of which serve to encourage and develop thinking. At times, therefore, flight can be a valid tactic to support one's learning. For instance, the classroom setting can prove to be unproductive if the lecturer is prone to deviating from the syllabus and telling irrelevant stories, whether as a result of incompetence or narcissism. In a situation of this kind, a student or the group as a whole might choose to disengage and to spend the time more fruitfully in private reading and reflection or in discussion with a group of friends. However, we have no evidence in our illustration that this was occurring.

Two aspects of the story point to distraction. First, the mass escape seems to have been a flight from the situation and from learning, not a flight into learning; second, it seems clearly to have been a group phenomenon not just an individual one. It would be too simple—in fact, it would miss the point—to say that the majority of the students involved had lost interest in the topic, the tutor, or learning more generally and so had deliberately chosen to be somewhere else. After all, the tutor and some individual students clearly *were* interested, as is evident from the one student's reaction to the tutor's question and from the fact that other students were also taking notes. Pockets of attention may still survive as oases in a desert of distraction.

It is important to note that the tension is reflected in the tutor's experience at the moment when she asked the class a direct question. Her intervention created a transition in the group and opened up a new dynamic in the room, albeit only briefly. The interaction that followed when the student took up her challenge prompts us to ask our questions again:

1. What patterns of interaction are manifesting in the group at this moment: dependency, fight–flight, and/or pairing?
2. Do these manifest interactions suggest that the group is giving attention to the truth and reality of the situation, or do they suggest a group characterised by distraction?

The questions are worth asking because the change of atmosphere suggests that something did shift as a result of the lecturer's question. At one level, the spark of interest might simply be attributed to a successful technique on the part of a teacher who was able to draw on many years' experience: change the mood by getting people involved. However, a focus on the nature of the interactions offers a different perspective.

The teacher's questions could be seen as an invitation to the group to interact in a different way. By asking a question she was inviting them to "come back", as it were; that is, to return from flight. If it had been successful we might then have seen evidence of the emergence of *greater dependency* (e.g., some questions asking for clarification, drawing upon the tutor's expertise) or perhaps of *fight* (e.g., a challenge to make the content more relevant, "I don't see how this applies to me/ the exam/my future work/etc."). In this particular situation, however, what we observe emerging is a *pairing* interaction. The evidence for this has two dimensions: first, there is an obvious exchange between two people (a pair); second, the exchange did indeed seem to inject into the group the emotion Bion associated with pairing; that is, hope—hope that something was about to happen.

Does this change provide evidence of attention or distraction? Unfortunately, it is difficult to be sure as it was so short-lived. Again, however, the experience of the tutor is illuminating: she reported being "brought to my senses with a jolt". This literally suggests a kind of awakening, which is also the term that she used to describe the impact of the question upon the group. In addition, by being put on the spot she experienced an impetus to think new thoughts, which is just what one would hope for from a learning experience of this kind. These are small indications of an encounter with truth: a real experience in the moment that evokes fresh thought and feeling.

On balance we believe that this was a genuine moment of opportunity for the group to move from distraction to attention. We say this because it accords with other experiences we have had of using Bion's insights, in what might be described as a technique: deliberately to use the forms of interaction to help a distracted group to shift attention back to its purpose. As was the case here, groups dominated by distraction tend to exhibit one form of interaction only. The technique involves making use of one of the *other* forms of interaction—in this example by invoking pairing in place of flight.

The alternative, of course, is to persist with the existing form of interaction and to try to use that to support attention. In this group, this would have meant persisting with flight and attempting to use it as a stimulus to attention. It is possible that this might indeed have been a constructive option. For example, the tutor might have thought something along the lines of, "The group seems to be distracted. They cannot concentrate on listening to me—I'll stop talking and give them time to reflect on the key learning points covered so far." As we suggested above, flight can support learning and in the right circumstances an intervention of this kind can help a group to get back on track as each individual reviews their own understanding and learning. However, the flavour of this story suggests that the most likely outcome would have been the opposite: it would simply have reinforced the currently dominant, distracted form of interaction and the students would probably just have gone on chatting to each other, texting, day-dreaming, and so on, rather than taking up the challenge. In a group that is already in touch with the purpose, such moments for reflection can be very productive, but members of a distracted group are much more likely just to flee in some other way.

Bion observed that when one mode of interaction dominates strongly it obscures the others, rendering them "inoperative". (1961, p. 102) Our experience confirms this. Instead of sticking with a distracted form of interaction, therefore, one is more likely to make a difference by using one of the other two. In this way, an intervention that mobilises dependence or pairing in a group dominated by fight–flight may have a containing or appropriately challenging effect. It can reduce the hold of the emotions underpinning the fight–flight response and so allow some of the energy tied up in distraction to be activated for the sake of the purpose.

It is possible that the tutor's question opened up for a moment an opportunity for the group to experience a significant shift in mentality—even though the moment did not last. The tutor told us later that she was annoyed with herself because she knew in retrospect what she'd like to have done. She wished she had picked up on the energy generated by her pairing interaction and pushed everyone else into doing the same sort of thing by getting them to turn to a neighbour and talk about what they had just heard. Even if what they actually talked about had little or nothing to do with the subject, at least they would be talking and so would be actively present. She might have reinforced this by asking people to move seats so that those who were on their own had someone to talk to. She had done this often enough in the past. The problem was that it did not even occur to her at the time. It seems likely that distraction was so pervasive that it was impossible in the moment for her to think clearly enough to access what she knew.

Of course, the benefit of hindsight is a wonderful thing; the truth is we just do not know if anything she could have done would have allowed the group to move into a state of attention or be encouraged to do so by the leadership of the tutor or one brave student. It is likely that their experience that morning was also influenced by the dynamics of the wider institution, which may have been too deeply set for anyone to make a real difference.

Managing a group through change

We have used the story above to introduce the three forms of interaction and also to show how difficult it can be to shift a group that is both dominated by distraction and stuck in one form of interaction. The following story, by contrast, illustrates the two aspects of this dynamic in a different way: first, the relationship between the forms of interaction themselves and, second, their impact in attention as well as in distraction. It shows the way a change in the form of interaction can affect the attention–distraction dynamic and also shows the forms of interaction themselves cooperating. This is one aspect of these dynamics that Bion did not discuss; that is, the way a group in a state of purposeful attention tends not to become stuck in one pattern of interaction but can mobilise one, two, or all three together in the service of the task.

The story involves a large-scale organisational change initiative where conflict was threatening to get out of hand. The resulting anxieties led to the emergence of fight as the dominant form of interaction to the point where it even seemed as if for many it had taken over as *the* purpose. This was clearly evident in the way individuals and groups attempted with some vigour to resist the proposed changes and aggressively to defend the current position. However, a shift from fight to pairing had the effect of also shifting the group mentality and successfully turned a distracted group into an attentive, cooperative one that was able to work towards a legitimate, common purpose.

In an effort to raise the quality of customer service the senior management team was planning an initiative across the whole organisation: this was about organisation-wide culture change and did not just apply to customer-facing departments. However, the customer service team, led by Adrian, was the first to have been selected to implement the initiative as a kind of pilot project.

Unfortunately, however, this was not an organisation prepared for change. There was an atmosphere of chaos and uproar, with claim and counter-claim, resentment, and resistance. Some staff felt attacked or patronised and demeaned by the insinuation that they did not know what good customer service was. They also felt the language management were using implied they were not working hard enough or even doing what was already being asked of them. Others, however, welcomed the proposals. Certainly, everyone seemed to have strongly held opinions about how things should and should not be done. As a result, even those who liked the idea often did not actually want to have anything to do with it in their own team. Open debate and discussion were almost impossible; only attack and counter-attack based on rapidly taken and rigidly entrenched positions. Whilst it was only "fighting-talk", this word "en-trenched" did have a First World War feel to it that seemed to capture the atmosphere exactly.

One day Adrian found himself talking about the situation over a cup of coffee in the company cafeteria with a colleague. The strength of emotion that emerged as he talked shocked them both. He described how he felt he was being badly treated in his role as customer service team leader. As his team had been picked for the pilot project he knew that how he handled this would have an impact on other teams and departments. At the same time he found himself having to deal with the strong, negative reactions of his own team members, many of whom he had worked with for years. Some of them were digging in their heels and asking for a better explanation of why they should do this. Importantly, they wanted to know why it was always them who were expected to change. They were refusing to have anything to do with the initiative and telling him to stand up for himself—although he felt this was really code for doing what they wanted. Their most commonly stated objection was that they had just put in place new procedures and relationships that really seemed to be working. So yes, they could see other people needed to change but they had only just finished sorting their new programmes. Why couldn't someone else do something for once?

Over coffee, Adrian mentioned an email he had drafted but not yet sent to the senior manager who was pushing him to be the first to trial the initiative. It made it very clear what he was and was not prepared to take on—and that this was a step too far. However, his colleague was not convinced. He said that in his experience emails just make tense and emotionally fraught situations of this kind worse; it's generally better to talk. And he said, "Why not just pop in to see this senior manager and ask for a chat?"

Adrian was a bit nonplussed. It had taken him long enough to accept that his team was right and to decide to put his foot down—and over an hour to write the email. But he could also see his colleague's point: he too knew the havoc emails can cause. So he decided to take up the suggestion and, much to his surprise, it worked. The senior manager believed in the initiative but also fully accepted how diffi-cult and demanding the situation was. She was supportive in relation to Adrian's concerns and active in offering help. Having broken away from the dynamic of attack and defence the two of them were able quickly and amicably to find common ground, to develop a plan, and to agree the resources needed to carry it out. The scheme was basically sorted in principle during that meeting, and when Adrian explained it to his team he was relieved by their readiness to take on the detailed planning and implementation.

A little while later he asked one of his team why she thought they had all been prepared to cooperate in the end and he was surprised by her response, "Sometimes it's just right to get on and do as you're told."

In order to show the influence of the forms of interaction in this exam-ple we will look at the story through three different lenses: the impact of the shift from fight–flight to pairing; the role of pairing; and the role of dependency. However, it is important to emphasise that in reality these elements were interrelated and we have only separated them for the sake of explanation.

The shift from fight–flight to pairing

Until his colleague pointed out the probable effect of another angry email, Adrian had not realised how deeply he had let himself become caught up in the prevailing culture of fight. His anger at what was being expected of him and his team had given him just the sense of righteous indignation that can make fight–flight seem to be an entirely rational and reasonable response, not an emotional one: "we" are right and "they" are wrong; "they" are the ones who cannot see what is going on and are being irrational and difficult to deal with; "they" are doing this to "us"; "they" never listen when we tell them their plans will not work; and so on.

So Adrian's reaction was typical of what was occurring generally at that time. There was no sense of agreement about anything, just a polarised "them-and-us" logic of right and wrong. As a result, the broader "we" of the organisation was getting nowhere, even though, ironically, most individuals acknowledged that things could not continue the way they were and that change was well overdue.

Standing back and asking the two key questions we introduced above produces two pretty unequivocal answers:

1. What pattern or patterns of interaction were manifesting in the group? Answer: predominantly *fight*.
2. Was this manifest fight interaction evidence of attention or distraction? Answer: *distraction*.

It was as if the organisation's actual purpose had been replaced by *fight* although it would probably have been given a less openly provocative definition such as, "to resist the proposed changes at all costs"—or at least to keep them out of my/our department/backyard.

Alongside the fighting there had also been several attempts to get negotiations going on the basic assumptions behind the change but their fate just provided further evidence of how strongly everyone was gripped by distraction. For example, several individuals and small interest groups had argued that to understand what the proposals meant for them they needed to agree a clear definition of purpose, "asking for a better explanation of why they should do this". All such attempts had failed. Even apparent appeals to reason seemed just to fuel the fire of emotion; they may have shifted the focus away from the changes and onto the purpose—but the fighting just continued on this new front.

It was all the more striking, therefore, that it just took a simple conversation over a cup of coffee with a colleague to open up a different possibility: a chat with the senior manager instead of a "clear"—that is, angry—email. It seems that the two pairing interactions involved—Adrian and his colleague, Adrian and the senior manager—were able to contain the general anxiety, antagonism, and resistance in a way that made hope possible. For Adrian, the senior manager, and the whole team, this hope proved stronger than the dominant atmosphere of fight. In the pairing with the senior manager neither party felt the need to put their energies into winning. Instead, they were able to cooperate in finding a solution that the senior manager could support and that Adrian believed he could convince his team to take on. It was remarkable how the shift in the form of interaction from fight to pairing seemed to enable a parallel shift from distraction to attention.

In the first pairing when Adrian met with his colleague it is possible that the mutuality of drinking coffee together may at some level have reflected symbolically the kind of shared exchange that lies at the heart of *friendship* as a pairing. Something about the friendly—or at least friend-like—nature of pairing appears to have de-personalised the interaction and so reduced the tension. As Tom Gilmore says about "productive pairs", they do not mobilise interpersonal relationships and intellectual understanding for personal advantage or pleasure but "in the service of the mission". (1999, p. 3)

However, a traditional not a modern view of friendship is implied by this experience. We tend to see friendship today as based on intimate, interpersonal sharing, "a vital safety-net providing much needed support and intimacy". (Spencer & Pahl, 2006, p. 210) Although the traditional understanding of friendship did not exclude such an experience of intimacy, it also embraced different and perhaps more challenging dimensions of the phenomenon. These are captured in Ralph Waldo Emerson's view of a friend as "a sort of beautiful enemy, untamable, devoutly revered", (1992, p. 104) and in William Blake's assertion that "Opposition is true Friendship". (1972, p. 157) So this was certainly a pairing—in public, in a café—but instead of a cosy chat it involved real conversation, which, as Emerson put it, "is the practice and consummation of friendship". (1992, p. 102)

The role of pairing

As we said above, Bion noticed how a pair can inspire a group with an air of hopeful expectation. The way this sense of hope plays out in group life depends, however, on whether the group is dominated by attention or distraction.

In attention, the hope generated by the presence of a pair translates into action; it becomes a "productive pair". The key is that the hope they generate motivates other group members to accept responsibility: the group does not leave it to the pair to do it for them. This is what seems to have happened in this case. Despite the strength of their resistance and their ongoing reservations, the rest of the team were persuaded by the outcome of the meeting and took on the practical details of planning and implementation.

When a pairing contributes to understanding the truth of the situation it can stimulate attention in the wider group in just this way, mobilising their energies in the service of the purpose. The hope the team experienced in this case was reality-based because it enabled them to be realistic not only about the situation but also about their shared strengths and weaknesses. At such moments group members can cooperate effectively in the present; as a consequence, they are able to pool individual and group contributions, value each other's areas of expertise, trust each other, speak frankly, and explore new ways of thinking, relating, and acting together.

This is in stark contrast to the effect when a pair emerges in a group dominated by distraction. The shared fantasy in such a group has two elements: first, that the pair has responsibility for the hope they have inspired; second, that the expectation they have evoked can only be fulfilled in the future. As a result, change in the present seems unnecessary and group members remain reluctant to take things on for themselves, trying instead to leave it all to the pair.

Bion expressed the situation even more strongly than this. He suggested that it is important for such a group to ensure that the hopes generated by the pair "do not materialize". (1961, p. 152) If they did it would imply that the pair had done their work; group members could therefore no longer rely on them, but would have to look their problems in the face and share responsibility for action in the present. A key hidden motivation for resisting responsibility in this way is that to become accountable would imply a need also to address the conflicts and anxieties that pushed the group into distraction in the first place. How much better to stay with the fantasy that the solution lies in the future and is the responsibility of the pair; then nothing needs to change or to be done *now*. In the story of the lecture at the beginning of this chapter, this was illustrated in the way the majority of those present gave no indication of a desire to get involved but were quite happy to leave the student–tutor pair to it.

Whether a group is in an attentive or a distracted state, therefore, a pair can embody for group members the belief that, however difficult their current situation may seem to be, they do nonetheless still have a future. In a group that is attentive to the truth, this moment of hope can be transformed into learning, development, cooperation, and reality-based action. Members of a distracted group, by contrast, hold onto the hope that they will be passively "saved" from their conflicts and anxieties by the pair or the outcome of the pairing. Their fantasy of reliance on the pair leads their energies to stagnate, (Bion, 1961, p. 128) and they remain stuck or paralysed as if fascinated only by the pair and what is going on between them so that any remaining confidence the group may have in its own capacities continues to leach away.

Bion did not associate expressions of pairing with friendship but with the idea of a sexual couple. He described how, in fantasy, group members hope the pair will produce a "child" to rescue them from a situation, which they feel unable to cope with as a result of "feelings of hatred, destructiveness, and despair, of its own or of another group ..." (ibid., p. 151) The group may imagine this "child" as a person—an external expert perhaps—or a saving idea or action, or the promise of a care-free future, all of which mean they do not have to look at their own part in creating the situation. This symbol of a child who will rescue the group is a powerful one, expressed in myths and religions across the world, from Moses in the bulrushes to King Arthur.

The difference of emphasis in relationship to time is reinforced in the two images of pairing: sexual reproduction stresses hope in a future "messiah" whereas friendship is all about the present because hope lies within the friendship itself, not in a future other. Friendship can even transform the experience of time, as when good friends meet after a gap of several years and find they simply pick up where they had left off; they have remained present to each other as if they had not been apart. The friendship tradition does not even view the pair as exclusive; instead, it understands a third person as being already present within the friendship. As the great Renaissance writer on friendship, Marsilio Ficino, put it, "there cannot be the two friends on their own, but there must always be three, the two men [sic] and God". (Ficino, 1975, p. 97)

The role of dependency and fight–flight

As we considered this story of the change initiative, we focused on fight–flight and pairing and on the way the shift from one to the other contributed a parallel shift from distraction to attention. Initially we did not notice that the third form of interaction, dependency, also played a role in the events. It was only later that we recognised how it came to work alongside pairing—and, indeed, fight and flight too—in the implementation of the initiative. The penny only dropped when we reflected on the comment, "Sometimes it's just right to get on and do as you're told."

This comment brought to mind a very simple image underlying the idea of dependency—the leader–follower relationship. Seen in this light it quickly became clear that the story involved several levels of dependency. The starting point was the decision by the senior management team to initiate a large scale organisational change. As the story makes clear, everyone could see some sense in their proposals even if they did not want to go along with them in their own area. The first level of dependency, therefore, involved Adrian's manager as the representative of senior management. Her task was to make sure that the first element of the plan was implemented. The second level involved Adrian and his team who had been identified as "guinea pigs", as one of them put it.

It is possible to imagine a culture in which everyone agreed with Adrian's team member that "it's just right to get on and do as you're told"—not only sometimes but *always*. This could be understood as a culture of dependency and it is likely that it would indicate a group dominated by distraction, blind followers who are unable to think for themselves. However, a group in attention might also create a culture of dependency; the difference is that they would be able to practice mutual dependency—in the sense that everyone is dependent upon the contribution of all group members for the cooperative achievement of the task.

It is clear from the story above that in a process of organisational change, senior managers cannot do it all on their own: they are dependent on those to whom specific tasks are delegated. This requires a culture not of unthinking dependency and obedience but one based on mutual listening and high quality dialogue, such as we observed in the pairings between Adrian and his colleague and then between Adrian and his senior manager. Finally, the quality of listening that emerged in the customer service team demonstrates how this attentive culture can pervade the whole group. In such a situation, mutual dependency requires that those in leadership listen attentively to everyone's opinions and only then make a decision—but on the understanding that then every individual group member will follow that decision whether or not it represents the views they had expressed earlier.

In the majority of organisations, however, this is not the case. Alongside the dependency of followers on leaders there is an equally strong tendency for the sequence to be broken. A fracture line opens when followers—at whatever level—do not agree with a decision and also do not feel they have been listened to, or feel put upon in some other way. At this point they are likely to shift from dependency to fight or flight and to resist doing what they have been told.

In his role as team leader, Adrian was caught in this tension between dependency and fight–flight. With one ear he listened to senior management, who had decided that his team should take on the required changes; with the other he listened to the team he belonged to and represented. It was only his colleague's comment about the email he had written that shocked him into realising just how clearly he had come down on the side of fight–flight and turned his back on dependency. Another way of putting his situation would be to say that he had lost touch with his sense of dependency on his own manager and had become dependent only on his team.

In all discussion of the forms of interaction, therefore, it is important to look at the way each can come to express either attention or distraction. Dependency does not mean unquestioningly doing what one is told to do and nor is its opposite blind resistance. Sometimes senior management do get it right, in which case following their lead represents attention. As ever, the key practice is the pursuit of truth.

It is possible that Adrian's pairing interaction with his manager led them both to a new experience of dependency. By agreeing to a face-to-face meeting they acknowledged each other's authority in their respective roles. The meeting then created a context where each could listen to the other attentively—and, as we have suggested, listening is the foundation stone of mutual dependency. Indeed, the root meaning of the word obedience (*ob-audire*) is to listen carefully and attentively. There is, however, something counter-cultural about the idea that taking up my role with authority can mean agreeing to do what I am told. Once Adrian and his manager had agreed on a course of action, Adrian then responded by expecting his own team members to act in a dependent way—to do as they were told. And they did.

Of course, the story did not end there. As with any example of change, organisational politics were never far from the surface. In Adrian's case, the decision to do as he had been told—or asked, perhaps—had a consequence he had not expected. Once he and the team had agreed to implement the new procedures, he found that he had to engage in a series of negotiations that he described euphemistically as "robust". This involved a sustained period in which he had to fight to create the conditions necessary for the new initiative to work, creating enabling structures for the team's work that many saw as being quite counter-cultural.

However, a striking feature of this time was that Adrian also remained keenly aware of not allowing fight–flight to obscure the importance of either pairing or dependency. For example, he made a point of meeting regularly with his senior manager, both formally and informally, and also with his colleague-friend over coffee. On the other hand, he also tried to make sure that his own team remained obedient by making a real effort to keep them in touch with senior management's thinking and with the overall progress of the initiative, and by listening to their reactions and to the reactions of colleagues from other departments.

This story illustrates how one characteristic of a group in a state of attention is that it can mobilise all three forms of interaction simultaneously. In contrast with Bion's view, (1961, p. 154) we believe this is a distinguishing feature of attention as a state of mind. A group that is distracted, by contrast, is likely to exhibit only one of the three patterns—such a group may move from fight to pairing or to dependency and back but it does not demonstrate the capacity to use two or all three at the same time. Effective group cooperation is facilitated by the potential to access all three forms of interaction in order to achieve the common purpose.

CHAPTER SEVEN

Learning the work of attention

Bion's sensitivity to the undercurrents of emotion and projection in groups meant that he was able to sense moments when he was being used by the group to perform a particular role—"manipulated so as to be playing a part, no matter how difficult to recognize, in somebody else's phantasy". (1961, p. 149) This awareness of unconscious group dynamics allowed him to spot both the group state of mind—attention or distraction—and the dominant mode of interaction. For example, he knew the group mentality was dominated by distraction and dependency when he sensed that group members expected him to solve every problem *for* them and to provide all necessary "nourishment, material and spiritual, and protection", (1961, p. 147) regardless of whether or not it was his role to lead. On such occasions, he felt that they saw him as a kind of god-like, fantasy figure: "I had become a kind of group deity; [...] questions were directed to me as one who knew the answers without need to resort to work ..." (1961, p. 148)

The final phrase is crucial: "without need to resort to work".

What is the work Bion refers to here? What is it that this all-knowing group deity does *not* have to do to be able to solve the group's problems—does not have to "resort to" because he or she *just knows*? What is the work that group members do not want to do for themselves?

It is the work of attention.

Our intention in writing this book has been to convey what we have learned—from Bion's writings, from others who have developed his ideas, and from our own experiences in groups—about the work of attention and about the forces that distract groups from working with attention. In this final chapter we would like to offer two final stories which describe developmental experiences whose purpose was to learn the work of attention. The first was a session designed specifically to teach a group of ten managers the approach that we have described in this book; the second describes one event in a group relations workshop, which is an experiential approach to learning about group dynamics that was influenced by Bion and his ideas.

These final stories—and our use of stories in general—recall Bion's warning against treating his ideas as a kind of game where we think we can stand on the outside looking in, as if removed from the group. Bion's concern, however, was to develop the capacity to be present in the moment: "I should add that it is much easier to believe one can see these phenomena in groups from which one is detached than in a small group in which one is actively participating. It is this latter experience which is the important one" (1961, p. 126). Detached observers can allow themselves the luxury of *believing* that they can see all kinds of things, but the immediacy of group membership is something else.

Consequently, Bion was interested in the tension between observation and involvement, theory and action. Ideas and their development are crucial but the present moment is the only place where the work of attention can happen. Movement in a group in which one is actively participating only happens when ideas and action play off each other as thinking-in-practice or practical intelligence. The two stories that follow give an indication of some of the demands involved in learning the work of attention in both of the forms we have described; that is, focused attention and evenly suspended, contemplative attention.

A group discussion

We had been asked to run a three-hour seminar on Bion's ideas as one element of a course for part-time mature learners—all managers or senior professionals in a range of public, private, and third sector organisations. The Masters module we were teaching on focused specifically on the unconscious dimensions of leadership. Having briefly introduced the ideas outlined in this book, we then asked participants to identify live issues in their work groups "back at the office". The following example was presented by the manager of a specialist training unit in a large organisation.

> The training unit had always seen itself as an important vehicle for creating a sense of identity and commitment to on-going change among staff across the organisation. However, in the face of a significant reduction in funding, senior management had decided to close the unit.

> Staff of the unit had been feeling for some time that they were under attack. Emotions were running high partly because it seemed that people elsewhere in the organisation had made a point of damaging the unit's reputation. The unit manager increasingly felt unable to give sufficient attention to meeting the training needs of new staff in particular because most of the time she felt she was just fighting for survival. Her team members felt beleaguered, absence through illness was at an unusually high level, and morale was low. She spent a lot of her time helping to resolve problems that she was sure her team members would once have managed on their own.

> At the same time, it appeared that everyone else in the organisation was doing something similar. The unit leader had met with a senior colleague in another department and he painted a similar picture: staff members were fighting their own corner and trying to avoid cuts or closure. There were other worrying signs of unhappiness: people were cancelling meetings, arriving late, not even turning up, or when they were actually physically present, just sitting in silence or absenting themselves by surreptitiously checking texts and so on.

> She was convinced that gossip and rumour had contributed significantly to damaging the unit's reputation and had been an important factor in senior managers' final decision to close it. There was a sense that they had been targeted for reasons that had little to do with the actual work of the unit or with the purpose of the organisation. The unit leader was seriously considering resigning, aware that several colleagues from other units had already left or decided to leave.

Using their initial understanding of the approach, the learning group immediately concluded that this organisation was an example of a group dominated by distraction—off track, out of touch—both the organisation as a whole and the training unit specifically. It seemed clear to them that the presenter's energies and those of the wider organisation were no longer being devoted to its purpose. In reaching this conclusion the participants were definitely influenced by the fact that they knew the presenter from working together on earlier modules and so had already learned something of her situation. They did not doubt her assertion that the unit she ran was integral to what the organisation stood for, and believed the loss of a sense of common purpose meant that the place and contribution of the unit had been forgotten too.

The presenter felt reassured and affirmed by the fact that others shared her perception of the situation. In a small learning group of this kind, whose members were used to sharing work experiences, this is probably not surprising. She also said she felt the approach had allowed her experience to be named in a different way.

However, we had framed the exercise as offering the possibility of going beyond analysis to action—and reassuring though it may be to have one's experience affirmed it does not necessarily change anything. Also we felt that the group might have missed something in assuming so quickly and unanimously that the organisation was in a distracted state; we wanted to test out whether on further consideration they would still feel that their immediate reaction had been accurate. After all, the conclusion that this was an example of distraction might well have been influenced both by the way the story had been told and by what they had heard in previous sessions—possibly also by recognising similarities to their own experience at work and jumping to conclusions.

To test their response and to guide them in interrogating the situation we asked them to consider the following questions based on the chapter themes, and to keep in mind their implications for both the training unit and the wider organisation:

- How can we be sure that this is indeed distraction not attention?
- What questions might help you to explore the important truths of this situation—particularly those that are unpalatable, such as the need for cuts?
- Is there any evidence in the account that the group is fulfilling its purpose?

- Do we see evidence of cooperation within the organisation and does the idea of groupishness, in particular of a "group animal at war", contribute anything to our understanding?
- What is the dominant form of interaction: dependence, pairing, or fight–flight?
- Does the manifest form of interaction shed any light on the first question—whether this is a group in attention or distraction?

For a group facing these ideas for the first time some of these questions were easier to work with than others. However, this was a learning exercise and the presenter's account did prove helpful in translating the basic ideas underlying the approach into more of a reality.

As far as the first question was concerned, the group stuck with their initial response. Everyone agreed that the unit and the wider organisation were both dominated by distraction. What really struck them—and it was central to their sense that this was distraction rather than attention—was the apparent lack of any discussion of purpose. They concluded that the presenter's energies were no longer being devoted to the purpose of the unit, despite the fact that they did believe she aspired to cooperate with the organisational purpose. Maybe it would have been too much to say anything else to a fellow student.

We should add that it is probably no great surprise to find that the presentation involved a work setting dominated by distraction. We had, after all, asked for an example of "a current work-based problem, which urgently needs dealing with". By asking for a problem, we increased the chances that the examples would involve distraction rather than attention. However, the discussion did make the students recognise in retrospect how many of the stories they had told each other about work involved a loss of purpose. They could see how the espoused purpose gets squeezed out by other things without discussion or explicit agreement and replaced by something else. They were shocked to recognise how, with a depressing regularity, the new purpose could be expressed as "to make money"—even in contexts where a broader sense of value might be expected, such as local authorities, education, medicine, and social work, all of which were represented in the group.

When we turned next to the forms of interaction evident in this story the students did not find the situation so clear-cut. At first, they played around with pairing and dependence and agreed that evidence could be found for both. For example, the presenter had talked about meetings she had held with a colleague from a parallel department. However, from her description group members were not clear whether this pairing had made any practical difference or had just become another opportunity to share their irritation about the situation they faced. In terms of dependence, they noted that the staff of the unit seemed to rely quite heavily on her as manager, expecting her to be able to sort out problems they would once have dealt with on their own authority.

However, after a somewhat frustrating and inconclusive discussion of pairing and dependency, someone remembered the third form of interaction, fight–flight, and everyone—especially the presenter—immediately agreed that fight was much nearer the mark. They wondered how they could have forgotten it because it seemed so obvious. From everything the presenter had described there seemed only to be space at work for rumour-mongering and back-stabbing, no room or energy for negotiation, compromise, sharing, and so on. What is more, no one seemed to be fighting *for* the organisation or even for their own unit—whatever they might have claimed to the contrary—but simply fighting *against* each other or fighting to survive. Someone said their own workplace was just the same: people talked all the time about the survival of the fittest.

One outcome of this discussion was to return the group to the question of attention–distraction and it confirmed them in their conviction that the unit was in the grip of distraction. The real purpose had been replaced by an as-if pseudo-purpose, which seemed to be encapsulated in the form of interaction itself: forget what you are really here for and save your own skin, beat the other, win—even though winning might actually mean losing if, for example, keeping "our" unit open led to the whole organisation failing for lack of funds.

At this point, the group felt they had nailed it: what the presenter had described was a unit gripped by distraction that found expression in fight as the dominant form of interaction between individuals and groups. For the sake of the exercise, however, they finally turned to the one element they had not discussed: flight. For some reason, they seemed less comfortable with flight than with fight. They seemed to think there was something wrong with running away. Right or wrong, however, they did see clear evidence of what looked like flight: absence through illness, cancelled meetings, lateness, people just sitting in silence, endlessly checking their phones, or not even turning up in the first place.

At this point, someone gently drew attention to the fact that the presenter herself was considering resignation and others in the organisation were doing the same. When pressed, she realised that she could recognise from her behaviour in the last few weeks just how much she had indeed begun to move from fight to flight. Until then, she had been quite dismissive of the people who were disengaging. The fact that she was now scouring the internet for job vacancies showed her just how much things had changed for her—although she had not thought of it as running away. The discussion reinforced for the group Bion's insight in coupling fight with flight, which up to then they had not fully understood.

The final issue raised in our questions concerned cooperation and groupishness. Because the story had been told from the presenter's perspective the group had most information about her and they clearly felt under considerable pressure to support her. However, the discussion of groupishness showed them that another side of the experience had rather gone missing, although there was no suggestion that the presenter had been deliberately misleading. Her personal needs and objectives—to have a career or to be seen as competent, for instance—may have been in conflict with the wider organisational pressures that had been so deeply affected by the external funding cuts. Her desire to leave in order to satisfy her individual needs was in direct tension with her desire and need for group membership. Maybe she was indeed a "group animal at war"—not only rather obviously at war with others in the group and with other groups but also at war with her own conflicted desires: should she stay and try to make the group work, or leave in order to free herself from the group demands, which were beginning to swallow up any sense she had of making an individual contribution?

We had used the approach to interrogate the presenter's experience of the situation—or it might be more accurate to put it the other way round: we had interrogated the approach by means of the story. However, we had not presented this merely as an academic exercise designed to create understanding for its own sake. Instead, the focus from the start had been on an example where something needed to be done, "a problem, which urgently needs dealing with". We were therefore left with a final question: could what we had learned about the approach help the presenter to intervene or behave differently?

One of the group members wanted to frame this in terms of an action plan, and this led to a discussion of the different levels at which she might intervene. Their first thought was that when she returned to work in a couple of days' time she could address the culture of distraction head-on by starting every meeting, negotiation, or written document with a restatement of the purpose. Of course, this would not guarantee that anything changed but it might have two useful effects. Like a splash of cold water on the face, her efforts to get people to focus on the common purpose might shock them into attention, reminding them what they were there for. However, if it made no difference then it might at least help her to decide whether to stay on or to leave. Either way, it might bring some clarity into a confusing situation.

So the group agreed distraction was the issue and they could see *in theory* that it might help to try and take that on directly. However, the idea did not generate any genuine feeling of hope. No one really believed it would have a beneficial impact on the presenter's experience at work; in fact, they thought it would probably just make things worse. Based on their own experience they thought that constantly repeating the purpose would just be experienced as irritating. They could all remember sitting in meetings and dismissing what someone said without even listening, while thinking to themselves, "Here he or she goes again …" They all thought that the fight culture was so embedded that any attempt to reinforce the purpose would be experienced as aggression not as a constructive way to behave. In particular, the presenter herself did not warm to the suggestion in any way. However well she did it she was convinced that it would almost certainly be counterproductive; even if she was explicit about *fighting for* the purpose others would just see her as *fighting*.

Things changed, however, when we shifted attention to another aspect of the approach: if addressing the culture of distraction head-on seemed likely only to make things worse, then might it make a difference to work instead with the forms of interaction? Did the group think that pairing or dependency might offer a way out of the impasse and stimulate a shift from distraction to attention? At this point, the atmosphere in the group changed. There was a new energy as they began to play with the alternatives and realised that there might indeed be other options. Everyone noticed the change and in the final review one of them said he was so familiar with the culture of fight–flight in his own workplace that it had been a real relief to see there might be other options.

Without hesitation the presenter immediately started to identify individuals with whom she thought she could create a bond, however temporary, that might be of mutual benefit. Two colleagues in particular sprang to mind: a senior manager and a peer in a related unit, who she knew was facing similar pressures. As we described in the previous chapter, the term pairing might sound a little grand for what may amount to no more than meeting for a cup of tea, but even something so ordinary can become the focus of hope for the future. In fact, the power of the intervention might lie in its ordinariness.

Some individuals in the group interpreted a pairing of this kind as a political act, a kind of alliance-building. However, they also recognised that in a fight culture pairing could offer not only a sense of hope, but also a kind of emotional containment that could create a different atmosphere by reducing the dominant sense of anxiety and fear. The presenter said she would not care whether it was seen as politics, friendship, or even an imaginary sexual pairing provided the outcome was constructive. As things stood, the atmosphere of attack and counter-attack was so intense that there was no space for creative thinking, no safe corner where a person could step back from the fray and see whether there was another way. Pairing seemed to hint at another possibility.

When the group turned their attention to dependency they also thought they could spot opportunities for action. In particular, it prompted one of them to suggest that it might make a difference if the presenter could think about changing her own view of herself and her role. Rather than seeing herself as the—rather passive—*manager* of the training unit maybe she could redefine her role in her own head as its active *leader*—like Boadicea resisting the Roman invasion, as another student put it.

The image was a striking one. Some group members thought it simply represented a slide back into fight but it led them to ask whether greater dependency would actually provoke fight or whether the two could work together. Maybe the problem was the choice of Boadicea as the model of a dependable leader. On another module they had come across the idea of servant leadership. Did taking up a leader role and actively encouraging dependency automatically mean she had to turn herself into a heroine who takes up arms on behalf of the oppressed?

The presenter instinctively identified with the idea of leading and serving her team at the same time. She felt that she could improve team members' self-image by supporting them and especially by making them realise what a good job she thought they had done in the past and could do in the future. At the very least, this might make the experience of coming to work more positive for everyone, particularly when others seemed determined to undermine the unit's reputation.

As a result of this discussion the group began to think about the idea of dependency a different way. They took up the idea of leadership as the embodiment of vision, and of vision as the expression of a group's common purpose. As leader of the unit the presenter could take a stronger lead—not in terms of fight but rather by defining the unique contribution of the training unit and emphasising its positive influence on the organisation overall.

At the end of the discussion it was pointed out that again we had not discussed flight as a form of interaction in its own right. Here too the group could see realistic options. First, it sounded as if whatever the presenter did her situation might simply be untenable. For her own sanity it might make sense just to leave. However, they knew this was unlikely to help the overall situation as she might not be replaced, which would mean there was no one left with the authority to represent the unit and support its staff. A second option was to frame flight as a strategic withdrawal. They suggested that stepping back or taking a time-out could be seen as an expression of attention rather than distraction, if it allowed her to return to the fray with new ideas, new options, or at the very least renewed energy levels.

The presenter could see the point of a strategic withdrawal of this kind. In fact, she said that in the past, when she had taken a holiday, she had often returned refreshed, and several group members recognised that attending modules on this course had been having a similar effect on them. By coming away from work for the regular three-day residential workshops, they not only found they returned with new ideas but also with their batteries recharged. So flight—for the moment—did seem to the group to be a potentially constructive response to the situation: temporary withdrawal in order to fight another day. They noted again how quickly military language can become part of the currency in situations of this kind.

During the coffee break following this discussion, the most senior manager present made what he called a confession. He said he had been feeling rather odd about the way he had learned to behave in meetings over the previous year or so, but that this session had allowed him to think about what he did in a different way. What made him feel bad was his nagging, guilty sense that he had been acting in a calculating or even manipulative way. However, he could now see that there was another way to think about what he did. In meetings he had learned to switch deliberately between fight and flight as the situation seemed to demand. So when he sensed a moment where he thought he could make a difference, he would use all his powers of persuasion, the authority of his role, and the strength of his personality to try to achieve what he wanted. On the other hand, when he sensed that the discussion was simply going around in circles and nothing he could do would have any effect, he simply did nothing. It often seemed to work but it left him feeling he was somehow playing with the other group members. Now he saw that what he did worked when it was in support of the purpose of the group he was in. As long as his choice of fight–flight behaviours was based on attention—that is, was in the service of the purpose and rooted in the pursuit of truth at that moment—then he felt justified in continuing.

Before we moved on to a second presentation, we took time to use the two key questions to analyse the way we had been working together during this session:

1. What patterns of interaction had manifested in the group: dependency, fight–flight, and/or pairing?
2. Did these manifest interactions suggest we were giving attention to the truth or reality of the situation and in line with the purpose of learning—or that we had become caught up in distraction?

This is another story that we will not elaborate upon except to say that it shares with this one a focus on *experience*. Learning the work of attention can never be done just in theory. In this respect, this chapter follows directly from the fact that Bion's learning came from his own experiences in groups. In the following and final story, we turn to an event specifically designed to create the conditions for participants to access their experience in a more direct way in order to help them expand their capacity for attention.

Developing the capacity for attention

Group Relations is the name given to a particular approach to experiential learning in groups, which evolved in the late 1950s at the Tavistock Institute in London (see Bibliography). The "Tavistock Method", as it is often called, was significantly shaped by the contribution of Bion's ideas that have formed the focus of this book. Over the intervening years it has developed as a powerful method of learning in groups, and many people have encountered Bion's ideas for the first time as a result of attending a group relations event of some kind. As the following story concerns events at a group relations workshop, it seems a fitting way to end our discussion of learning the work of attention.

As the phrase experiential learning suggests, the focus of these workshops is on learning from direct experience within the workshop— or "conference" or "working conference", as they are often called. The approach to learning is not based on teaching, as that is normally conceived—there are no lectures, seminars, or readings—but on direct experience in the here-and-now of the workshop itself. An experience of this kind can generate a particular energy and depth of learning because the way of working makes it hard to indulge in the kind of defensive behaviours that often accompany learning, such as hiding behind intellectual arguments or competing over who knows the most—or the least.

In this way the group relations approach plunges participants into an immediate experience of their ability to cooperate in the pursuit of truth, and they experience the tensions inherent in human groupishness. Group members can quickly find themselves thrown into a state of profound self-questioning that puts their capacity for attention to the test. The anxieties that are provoked can easily lead to the group being swamped by distraction vividly expressed in the way dependency, fight–flight, and pairing emerge to dominate their interactions.

In a group relations workshop, participants are offered the opportunity to experience the ways in which they take up their roles in a variety of group settings—small, large, and inter-group. Some of these events focus on internal group dynamics, others on the relationships that develop between groups and the effect inter-group contacts have on the internal dynamics of the sub-groups. There are also sessions devoted to reflection on the here-and-now experience of these different events and on the learning that may be emerging. These reflective sessions include reviews in which participants look *back* at what has happened in order to help digest the experience itself—and look *forward* in preparation for later events or for the next day. Finally, application sessions enable participants to focus on applying the learning from the workshop as a whole to their work roles.

The focus of study in the here-and-now events is the group-as-it-is-in-this-room-at-this-moment with all the emotions, ideas, events, comments, and silences that are there. It is not a space for reflection on what happened in an earlier event or in the break or on what goes on in groups at work, and so on, although inevitably these do also become the focus of attention. The creative—and, it has to be said, unsettling—element of the experience is that those aspects of everyday group life which are normally not given much, or indeed any, attention tend to become the object of awareness; for instance, the significance of speaking or not speaking, of time boundaries and incidents of lateness, of where people choose to sit, of the roles people take up or are given, and, for each individual, of their own more or less hidden feelings and thoughts and what to do with them. The potential for deep learning in these events comes from the way issues of this kind become available *for the work of attention*—not as detached, theoretical issues but in the context of a cooperative group experience.

The staff members at a group relations event are present in the role of consultant, as they are called, rather than as group members, facilitators, managers, or teachers. The consultant role involves noting aspects of the process, which they think group members might be avoiding or might not even have noticed, and offering hypotheses about the process as they experience it. The consultant's role is to point to the truth in the moment as they see it in relation to the purpose of the workshop and the particular task of the session.

The following story is taken from a five-day group relations workshop. The common purpose—the aim of the workshop—had been defined as follows: "to develop participants' awareness and understanding of complex group dynamics and to learn to work in groups more effectively". In what follows, we recount a moment at the start of the first large study group, when the group fell quickly into distraction. In terms of the forms of interaction, this distracted state manifested first as dependency and then fight–flight. The story, which we tell in two parts, goes on to show how the capacity for attention can develop even after an unpromising start.

The large study group

It is towards the end of day one. Before the final review of the day in small groups there is a one-hour "large study group", which comprises all thirty-four participants and three of the seven staff members, seated together in one room. The task of this event is designed to contribute to the overall workshop aim in the context of a large group. It is expressed as being, "to study the group dynamics in the here-and-now of a large group."

There is a good deal of chat as everyone sits waiting for the event to begin. At 5.30 p.m., the third and final staff member enters the room, closes the door and takes his seat. Most people have probably noticed his arrival because he has had to pick his way between the seats to the empty chair right in the centre of the room. However, it is unlikely that many people realise his entrance was timed to mark the time boundary at the start of the event, and the general level of conversation continues as before.

After a brief pause he welcomes everyone, reminds them that this is the first of four large study groups—at which point everyone falls silent as they realise things have started—and states the task of the group as it is written in the course handbook: "To study the group dynamics in the here-and-now of a large group."

Almost immediately, someone asks him to repeat the task—on the face of it a rather innocuous request. In normal life, rather than a study event of this kind, it's the kind of thing that happens all the time.

He says nothing—in fact he does not respond at all. The resulting tension in the room is palpable.

In a setting where the task is to study the group in the here-and-now, an apparently simple request to repeat what has just been said can take on a particular significance, reminiscent of the impact of lateness and the missing chair in the story we told at the end of Chapter One. In a similar way, a request of this kind has the potential to highlight things that might be missed in an everyday work group. After all, something had just happened "in the here-and-now of a large group". Just to respond in what might be considered a "normal" way by repeating the task as requested might have run the risk of missing something about this particular interaction in this group at this moment. It might, for instance, have distracted attention from the only just emerging relationship between participants and between participants and staff, or from the role and importance of questions for members of *this* group.

Was the question ordinary or did it echo Bion's description of the way a distracted, dependent group directed questions at him "as one who knew the answers without need to resort to work"? (1961, p. 148) Did the consultant in this instance feel comfortable with the question or did he sense that he had instantly been turned into a fantasy group deity, "manipulated so as to be playing a part, no matter how difficult to recognize, in somebody else's phantasy"? What can be learned from the consultant's silence?

One possibility is that he was engaged in the inner work of attention. Clearly, instead of remaining silent he might simply have answered the question—on the assumption that a question is just a question and that the person who asks it has the right to an immediate answer. If he had done so everyone might have been able to ignore the meaning and impact, emotional and political, of *this* question in *this* large group at *this* moment. If he had just repeated the task this might have allowed everyone to believe that all that was involved was a straightforward request for information. While at one level this may have been true, it would have ignored other possibilities and might not have matched the truth of the consultant's experience in the moment. For example, this apparently uncomplicated request for information might also have represented a more or less conscious attempt to experiment with the relationship between the group and the consultants by trying to get one of them to *do* something—a testing of power relations in the group. If this were the case then what seemed like an innocuous request also offered an opportunity to learn something more general about what it can mean to question an authority figure—at that moment but also in groups and organisations more generally.

A number of questions need to be asked in order to pursue the truth of this moment. Were the participant's request and the consultant's silence based on distraction or attention? Did they represent an avoidance of an uncomfortable moment or the search for truth? Was the question a *real* request for information or did it represent some kind of fantasy in the minds of participants—whether about relations in the group, about the purpose, about group roles, or about power relations and authority? And did the consultant make his decision not to respond in the expected, normal way because he had not heard the question properly, because he was behaving in a controlling way, because he was confused or just plain rude, or maybe because he felt the interaction in the moment offered an opportunity "to study the group dynamics in the here-and-now of a large group"?

Whatever the truth may be there is little doubt that the request took on a particular significance coming as it did almost the instant after he had read out the task. Right at the start of the session it plunged everyone directly into the heart of the task of the event and the workshop. It seems that it really did present a group dynamic for study: a particular experience of group behaviour—as it happened—not in any large group but this one. Or, to frame the moment in terms of the overall workshop aim, it offered a specific opportunity "to develop participants' awareness and understanding of complex group dynamics", as a result of which they might "learn to work in groups more effectively".

So how *did* the group behave at that moment? Well, as we have said, the request clearly had an effect on the consultant because he did *not* do the usual thing and read the task again—usual, that is, in ordinary social situations. Instead, he remained silent and the impact of his silence was quite shocking for the participants: many were visibly angered and seemed to feel insulted. However, it should be said that no one actually knew *why* he had not responded in the expected way and nor did anyone ask him what he was thinking. In group relations, events staff behaviour is the focus of keen attention and is often experienced as less than helpful. In this instance the consultant may have been caught somewhat unawares, knocked a bit sideways by the suddenness of the reaction, or he may have been half expecting it, which may have led to his behaving rather formally, or "stiffly" as someone put it, and as a result being experienced as withholding.

On the other hand it was evident to anyone who looked around that there were plenty of others in the room who could have helped clarify the matter. *Everyone* had a copy of the task in their papers for the workshop and so could have read it for themselves before arriving at the session. In addition, the workshop aim and the task of every event had been emphasised in every session throughout the day. So the idea of having a group purpose and working to a task did not come out of the blue. One participant, sitting only two seats away from the consultant, had her folder open at the relevant page and could have responded to the request by reading out the wording of the task, or those sitting near her could have asked her to do so. It was a little odd that everyone appeared to have arrived so unprepared and seemed so deskilled— as if somehow they had lost their minds! These are all indicators of emotional reactions that might have led the consultant to believe that the group was in a distracted state.

The three consultants were also influenced by the fact that they had given considerable thought to the opening of this first large study group. Indeed, in their planning sessions they had specifically discussed whether or not to read the task out at all. They had eventually decided to do so in an attempt to help participants engage more easily with an event that was likely to be experienced as quite unfamiliar. They had agreed that this particular group might think it rather weird if the consultants just came in, sat down, and waited for something to happen, as is often the case in a group relations workshop. They felt that group members would probably find it easier to engage in the session if the start was marked in some way, and had decided that reading out the task would be appropriate.

So it seems that more was involved at that moment than just impoliteness or unhelpfulness on the part of the staff—although somehow their attempt to be helpful had turned out quite differently. This may not be surprising. The inevitable tensions and anxieties generated by joining any new group mean that the kind of confusion faced by the participants at the start of this workshop is not at all uncommon. The effect of these strong emotions is often to provoke distraction and this can be particularly clear in a group relations event. In this case, it is reflected in the experience of being unable to think. (Bion, 1961, p. 95)

It is worth saying that the participants were aged from their mid-20s to mid-50s and came from a very diverse set of educational, social, national, and racial backgrounds. A few were unemployed but most were in employment and held a wide range of roles and responsibilities in the public and private sectors. And yet somehow in the heat of the moment the group as a whole seemed to lose touch with their considerable experience and competence. They seemed to be thrown into a state of extreme dependency where all that mattered was to know exactly what the task was and *the only route to this knowledge* seemed to be the consultant who, ironically enough, had just reminded them what it was.

In terms of the form of group interaction, this moment seems therefore to have been one of dependency. This may have been sparked by what participants experienced as a failure on the part of the consultant to provide them with a safe container; that is, a reliable place where they could with confidence take the risks that are always associated with new learning. It was as if this group of thirty-four experienced people who were all used to working in groups every day, managing teams, leading projects, dealing with very difficult clients, and some handling enormous budgets, were saying, "If we cannot even get a response from this person then how can we possibly learn anything? We are dependent on the staff. Without them we don't even know what our task is. We don't know what to do …" At the same time they were somehow able to ignore the fact that each one of them actually had direct access to this information. The situation matched closely Bion's description of a group gripped by distraction and dependency, yearning for a leader who would provide them with "nourishment, material and spiritual, and protection" (1961, p. 149)—but left with one who in their experience was failing to do so.

These events raise many questions: Were the dominant modes of distraction and dependency set up by the overall context of the programme and the way of working? Did the staff's behaviour create dependency as the dominant mode of interaction? How much was the situation influenced by participants' past experience of school and of other educational or training events? Was there some reason why the group slipped so quickly into dependency, rather than fight–flight or pairing? Was dependency the dominant form of interaction or does the sense of anger also suggest the presence of fight?

Before turning to what happened next we would like to pause to consider what these events might tell us about the dynamic of dependency and its relationship to attention and distraction.

From distraction to the work of attention

At one level, a certain degree of dependency on the staff team was clearly to be expected. As they had been responsible for creating the programme for the workshop, they could be expected to know what they were doing in terms of the structure and the way of working. Dependency of this kind might be described as healthy dependency and its presence was acknowledged by the workshop director in sending out a brief welcome letter that gave times and directions for the start and some preliminary thoughts about the work. Each participant had also received a course folder on arrival with full details of the timings of events, the task for each session, lists of names, and so on. On the other hand, however, the participants also knew a great deal that the staff could not hope to know—about each other, about the level of their own understanding, about their hopes and expectations, and about their own experiences in groups. So the staff knew more about some things and the participants were more knowledgeable about others, and it was to be hoped that something creative would emerge through an exploration of these differences.

If the participants had experienced all of this as sufficiently reliable and containing then would events have taken a different turn at the start of the large study group? We can only speculate of course but if, for instance, everyone had arrived at the session having read the pre-course material then they might already have felt confident in their knowledge of the task. As a result, they might have experienced the consultant's words as a useful acknowledgment that the session had started and a reminder of what they already knew, and there would have been no need to ask him to repeat what he had just said. It is likely that there would still have been a high level of tension and discomfort but the confirmation that they were in the right place at the right time might have helped them to see that these awkward feelings were more or less inevitable given the novelty of the setting, the fact of meeting each other in a new context, and so on.

Things might also have turned out differently if one of the other participants had been the first to respond to the request for a re-reading of the task. For example, the woman who had her folder open at the relevant page—and there may have been others—might simply have said something like, "I've got the task here. Let me read it out." Or one of her neighbours might have said, "Is that the programme you're looking at because I've left my folder outside? Would you mind reading the task out again? I didn't quite get it." Or the person who had asked the question might have explained that her hearing was not good so she simply had not heard what had been said. She might then have apologised for sitting at the back and asked if someone would mind swapping seats with her. Each of these alternatives—and there are of course many others—would have represented very different examples of "the group dynamics in the here-and-now of a large group".

None of this would have denied the presence of dependency. However, the flavour of the experience would have been quite different. First, participants might have experienced the staff as reliable. For example, they had clearly thought carefully about the structure and aim of the workshop and the individual events and also about the participants; also the event had started on time, in the right room and with a chair for everyone, and it was reassuring that the task that had been read out used exactly the same wording as in the folder. Many of those present would have known from their own experience how much work goes into planning a three-day event of this kind. Second, the participants might also have experienced each other as reliable by the way they interacted and realised they could depend on each other and not just on the staff. As a consequence, everyone might have felt they had the freedom in their roles as participants or consultants to explore the significance of their behaviour. In other words, the group interactions could still have been characterised by dependency but rooted in attention and not as an expression of distraction.

Under these circumstances the group might have realised, "Wow! We're here 'to study the group dynamics in the here-and-now of a large group' and look what we just did! We immediately handed over responsibility to the consultant to tell us what we're here for—even though we knew already. We gave up our own authority and handed it over to someone we see as an authority figure here—although it's been made perfectly clear from the start that they're not here to teach us or define our learning for us!" Participants and staff together might have tried to understand where this deferential, heavily dependent experience of authority had come from. Was it a result of their experiences of home, school, university, or the workplace? Was it perhaps a reflection of gender relations in society more widely, in view of the fact that it was a woman who had asked the question of a man? And what had the staff done to trigger this behaviour? The resulting discussion might have led to insights into their experience of dependency in their everyday work roles.

Clearly dependency is neither good nor bad. None of the forms of interaction is good or bad *in itself*; they are just a fact of group life. In this example, it seems that by the time the first large study group took place a kind of emotional overload had already built up during the day so that the way this session started was enough to tip the group into distraction. Maybe they were already distracted. What is certain is that in the moment they lost sight of the task—study—and were thrown instead into demanding an immediate answer to—or way out of—the difficulties they were experiencing. The search for truth was taken over by the search for the comfort of an answer. The group mentality was dominated by distraction; the form of interaction was dependency.

At a more general level, this story also illustrates why the group relations approach to learning can be so powerful: it exposes the nature of what is happening in the here-and-now in a way that makes it hard to ignore. As a result, the dynamics can be easier to see and so to study and to learn from, but only if members of the group can retain a capacity for attention that enables them to go on thinking. At this particular moment in our illustration, members of the large study group do not seem to have retained this capacity for attention. However, over the five days of the workshop a great deal of significant learning resulted from the ongoing interactions in the group. The raw experience of distraction in the first large group session contributed significantly to their learning when it could later be placed in the wider context of the whole workshop. In our experience of the group relations approach to learning this is not untypical: group members can easily be overpowered by a desire to judge experience immediately as right or wrong, good or bad. One strength of this kind of workshop is that it offers a container where rapid, even instant, judgments can be scrutinised; there is time to explore other ways of experiencing and understanding what we know by holding back from such judgments and maintaining a neither-right-nor-wrong, neither-good-nor-bad mentality.

In the ebb and flow of group life, distraction and attention, the pursuit of truth, cooperation, clarity of purpose, dependency, fight–flight and pairing, all exist in potential in every group at every moment. Different configurations of these elements will dominate at any particular moment. Sometimes they last for a lengthy period but there will also be rapid and sometimes frequent swings between them. Such movements are not only evident between attention and distraction but also in a greater or lesser dedication to the pursuit of truth, in the level of cooperation, in a more or less clear sense of purpose, and in the way in which the forms of interaction replace each other or work together.

This large study event began in a state of distraction dominated by dependency as group members tried to escape what they experienced as an extremely uncomfortable situation—and anyone who has attended such an event will know just how difficult this experience can be. In some ways the question that was asked, and the group's response to it, felt like an attack on the whole event, including on staff—more like fight than dependency. And the initial focus of the participants' exasperation and anger was clear: it was the consultant—the authority figure—who they saw as the leader and who had indeed taken a lead by marking the start of the event as he had.

The gradual shift from distraction to attention that took place during the workshop seems to have been connected to two developments. First, the staff team deliberately experimented with *pairing* as an alternative form of interaction to dependency. They tried not to behave as leaders in relation to followers but rather as equals who wanted to help. At times they expressed this by behaving the way friends might behave looking after the participants. For example, when it turned out that no water had been delivered in the room set aside as a social space for participants, staff members found the missing bottles and cups and took them to the room. In doing so, they acted in the role of manager rather than consultant and demonstrated an appropriate level of care and attention. They also kept to time and strove to maintain a focus on task no matter what happened. As a result, an increasing number of participants began to realise that staff were not playing games with them but were attending carefully and seriously to what was happening. The interpretations and observations offered by consultants were increasingly experienced as supportive of the learning process.

Second, and partly as a result, group members began to take up their own authority in situations where leadership of some kind was required. For instance, if someone knew the answer to a question then they might say so rather than expecting it to come from the staff. This could take the simple form of an action such as opening a window if the room was too hot or closing it if it became too noisy. In this way, members were able to get in touch with their own potential to contribute to the purpose and the work of the group through their own attentiveness.

We shall return now to events in the first large study group, in order to see how things turned out.

The large study group (continued)

The moment when a consultant in a group relations workshop chooses to remain silent, failing to respond in the expected way, can be a startling and uncomfortable experience. The sense of affront was palpable as well as shocking in the speed and force of its appearance. The target was clearly the consultant at the centre of the room. In his mind, his (apparent lack of) response was an attempt to keep to the role of consultant by holding to the task; that is, by drawing attention to behaviour in the group. He responded to the experience of being asked a question by not responding directly to it and so he set up a tension that was tricky both for him and for group members. Instead of accepting the fantasy of dependence that turned him into "the one who knows", (Lacan, 1979, pp. 232–233), he appealed to their capacity for attention and tried to return them to a sense of their own inner authority. However, this way of engaging with the task just seemed to make the situation more difficult and confusing.

> The consultant does not reread the task as requested, but he responds shortly afterwards by offering a hypothesis about what is happening in the group. There is a moment of silence after he speaks this second time.
>
> However, the moment does not last. The atmosphere quickly shifts from questioning to attack. First of all, some group members turn on the consultant who has refused to do as he has been asked. Their vigorous attacks express a sense of outrage and offence that he could behave in such a way. It seems that in the minds of the participants the three consultants have become the enemy. At the same time, many participants take flight into silence and so protect themselves by "disappearing".
>
> Towards the end of the session, a fresh wave of indignation is released in the group and one participant launches a personally insulting attack on the withholding consultant. All hell seems to break loose. Several members express their anger, some voicing outrage at what the participant has said, while others are shocked by the perceived passivity and ineffectuality of all three consultants. Some attack the group member for the personal nature of his attack whilst others defend him. Some attack the consultants and how they are performing their roles, others attack the way of working. By contrast, several participants freeze in silence and others literally flee by getting up and walking out of the room a few minutes before the session ends. Several people make it clear that they do not think they will be able to come back the next day.

As is probably clear from this description, the anxiety in the room at that moment was so heightened that study was almost impossible. This experience of losing the ability to think, whether as group member or consultant, is often a distinguishing feature of the experience of distraction. It includes the inability to remember what the purpose is. In this session, for example, it was vividly and very physically obvious at the end of the first large study group that the group had lost touch with the task. In Bion's words, it seemed to have "changed its purpose": (1961, p. 31) the focus on study and understanding had gone as people either tried to *force* each other to behave differently or tried to *escape* the situation. In other words, the dominant form of interaction had very colourfully transformed from dependency into fight–flight. Distraction, however, continued to dominate.

It is probably worth saying something about the word "study" in this context, because some participants initially found it misleading. Study can suggest a certain detachment, reminiscent of Wordsworth's "emotion recollected in tranquillity". (Stafford, 2013, p. 111) However, an experiential approach to the study of group dynamics relies on *immersion in* the experience, not detachment from it. Without immersion in the experience, study becomes a merely intellectual exercise and any learning remains in the realm of ideas and knowledge rather than being translated into behavioural change. The kind of experiential learning represented by the group relations approach tries to keep together experience and reflection on experience, in a way that can provoke fresh insights into behaviour and lead to learning and change.

Does the description we have given of this study group do justice to the nature of the learning that took place and the electric texture of the experience? The personal insult directed at the consultant could not be defended as a joke, although some people did try to do so. Ultimately however, the focus of attack seemed to be less the consultants and more the group relations way of working that they represented. If the consultants allowed personal insults of this kind then how could the event possibly be described as study? How could anyone be expected to have the mental and emotional detachment necessary to study the dynamics of this large group in the here-and-now? How could such a highly charged situation possibly be expected "to develop participants' awareness and understanding of complex group dynamics and to learn to work in groups more effectively"? At that moment most people would have agreed they were indeed having an experience of "complex group dynamics" but in a way that was entirely indigestible and certainly could not support learning. How could participants be expected to "learn to work in groups" when a few people were so dominant that no one else could even take part properly? And, if study and understanding were impossible how could anyone "learn to work in groups more effectively"?

In the mêlée some people directly and angrily confronted the participant who had insulted the consultant while some defended him and others confronted the consultants as a group. Two or three individuals left in distress. An outside observer would have been forgiven for thinking the purpose at that moment was either to exact revenge for the attack or to mobilise others into action against the attacker—or to escape the situation altogether. No one would have deduced from the evidence available that the purpose was "to study the group dynamics in the here-and-now of a large group". The group seemed to be acting out their aggression, not studying.

There is, however, more to be said. After all, there is no doubt that something did happen and that it was a lived example of group dynamics. Maybe if the group had felt able to study these events in a coolly detached way then that would have been less authentic than the fight–flight reaction that was evoked. People certainly did not let the insult go unnoticed or treat it as if it were normal and acceptable. One element of the highly emotional response was that it provoked a principled defence by some participants of the staff team's legitimate authority and also of the personal authority of group members.

We have emphasised the importance of Bion's belief that attention and distraction are present in potential *in every group at every moment*. The desire for it to be otherwise is perfectly understandable; that is, the desire to create the perfect group, where everything just works. However, this is a utopian fantasy in the literal sense of utopian: that there is "no place" where it can be found. The perfect group, where everything works comfortably and to plan, simply does not exist except in imagination and desire.

So distraction manifesting as dependency was certainly dominant at the start of this large study session, and distraction in the form of fight–flight was dominant as the session ended. But this was not the end of the workshop, nor was it the final large study group. In fact, it was not even the end of the first day. The large study group was followed after a short break by the first of the "small review groups" with which each day ended. Membership of these was the same as for the "entry groups" with which the workshop had started.

The purpose of the review groups was to provide "the opportunity to reflect on your experiences and learning from the workshop and the roles you have taken so far." There is no doubt that these groups had a significant impact on the participants. They used them to process some of the emotions experienced throughout the day, including in the large study group. A second reflective space was scheduled for the start of the second day. Called a "morning meeting", it offered both participants and staff the opportunity "to raise any issues relating to the workshop and any overnight thoughts." The participants and the staff team did indeed make use of this opportunity to address very directly issues and emotions left over from the previous day. This included the setting of a clear boundary by the workshop director in relation to what constituted acceptable and unacceptable behaviour in relation to personal comments of the kind that had been made the previous day. Partly as a result of this processing, everyone was present at the second large study group directly after the morning meeting, despite the strong statements made by some about not returning.

The impact of these two reflective sessions illustrates the way in which the constant tension between distraction and attention can be worked with. Two elements seem to have been crucial. The first element is the nature of the containing structures; that is, (1) not only the structure of the workshop, which integrated experiential and reflective spaces or events, but also the ability of staff to remain in and work at their roles and; (2) attention to the pursuit of truth in the moment, cooperation guided by purpose, and a readiness to work actively with the group dynamics as they emerged, which was demonstrated, albeit imperfectly, by the staff and participants alike.

The work of attention

Bion's ideas have been our starting point as we have explored the work of attention but he never claimed they were the final word on the subject; quite the opposite in fact. Throughout *Experiences in Groups* he gently but insistently invites the reader to test out his ideas. In the second paragraph of the book, for example, he states that he has included the first chapter, the earliest of the nine to have been published as a journal article, "because it throws light on the origins of my belief that this approach merited further trial", adding that he included the last chapter "because it summarizes conclusions that I would like to have taken further, and that others might like to develop". (1961, p. 7) In the book's final sentence, he again challenges us as readers to decide for ourselves whether or not his ideas on group dynamics give meaning to the phenomena we can observe in the course of our daily lives as members of groups.

Bion never did return to write exclusively about group experience and dynamics. Indeed, as Armstrong has put it:

> Bion didn't think much of *Experiences in Groups*. In a letter to one of his children he comments wryly on its critical reception compared to his later published work: "the one book I couldn't be bothered with even when pressure was put on me 10 years later, has been a continuous success". (Armstrong, 2005, p. 11)

In an interview towards the end of his life, Bion reacted strongly to the suggestion that many people "regard it as a definitive piece of work", saying, "That would be a pity. The book is not the final view, and I urge people working with groups to make it out of date as soon as possible." (Banet, 1976, p. 284)

He did, however, concede that "certain basic things in *Experiences in Groups* are worth retaining". (Ibid.) One of these, in our view, is the importance of a dynamic interplay between theory and action—recognising that knowledge and practices from the past should not be lazily applied in the present. Hence his comment about the danger of using ideas in a defensive way: "We learn these theories—Freud's, Jung's, Klein's [we could add, *Bion's*]—and try to get them absolutely rigid so as to avoid having to do any more thinking." (Bion, 1978, p. 6)

Bion's ideas have not saved us from having to do any more thinking—far from it! Rather they have helped us to acknowledge the uncomfortable reality that so often the dynamic of distraction can make thinking all but impossible. However, he has also shown us that it is essential to pursue truth in the moment with perseverance, putting our knowledge into practice in the here-and-now of group life—when "under fire", to use his metaphor. Bion's focus on the dynamics and impact of distraction has tended to obscure the fact that he also had great faith in the potential for attention to triumph over distraction "in the long run"; (Bion, 1961, p. 135) that is, to support cooperative action between individuals as they work together to achieve their shared purpose.

REFERENCES

Alford, F. (1994). *Group Psychology and Political Theory*. New Haven: Yale University Press.

Alford, F. (2004). Small groups and big nations: Politics and leadership from the perspective of the small study group. In: S. Cytrynbaum, & D. A. Noumair (Eds.), *Group Dynamics, Organizational Irrationality, and Social Complexity: Group Relations Reader 3* (pp. 5–22). Jupiter, FL: A. K. Rice Institute for the Study of Social Systems.

Armstrong, D. (2005). *Organization in the Mind: Psychoanalysis, Group Relations, and Organizational Consultancy—Occasional Papers 1989–2003.* R. French (Ed.). London: Karnac.

Banet, A. G. (1976). Interview: Anthony G. Banet Jr., interviews Wilfred R. Bion, major theorist of the Tavistock approach. *Group and Organizational Studies, 1*: 268–285.

Barnhart, R. K. (Ed.) (1988). *Chambers Dictionary of Etymology*. Edinburgh: Chambers.

Binyon, L. (1914). Ode of remembrance, in "For the fallen", poem first published *The Times*, 21 September 1914.

Bion, W. R. (1961). *Experiences in Groups*. London: Karnac [reprinted London: Routledge, 1989; London: Brunner-Routledge, 2001].

Bion, W. R. (1962). *Learning from Experience*. London: William Heinemann Medical Books [reprinted London: Karnac, 1989].

Bion, W. R. (1965). *Transformations*. Abingdon: Fleetwood Press [reprinted London: Karnac, 1991].

Bion, W. R. (1967). *Second Thoughts*. London: William Heinemann Medical Books [reprinted London: Karnac, 1987].

Bion, W. R. (1970). *Attention and Interpretation*. London: Tavistock [reprinted London: Karnac, 1984].

Bion, W. R. (1978). *Four Discussions with W. R. Bion*. Strath Tay, Perthshire: Clunie Press.

Bion, W. R. (1990). *Brazilian Lectures: 1973 São Paulo, 1974 Rio de Janeiro/São Paulo*. London: Karnac.

Bion, W. R. (1991). *A Memoir of the Future*. London: Karnac.

Bion, W. R. (1994). *Cogitations* (extended edn). London: Karnac.

Blake, W. (1972). *The Marriage of Heaven and Hell*. In: G. Keynes (Ed.), *Blake: Complete Writings with Variant Readings* (corrected edn, pp. 148–160). London: Oxford University Press.

Brecht, B. (1966). *Der Jasager und der Neinsager: Vorlagen, Fassungen und Materialien*. Frankfurt am Main: Suhrkamp.

Burton-Christie, D. (1993). *The Word in the Desert: Scripture and the Quest for Holiness in Early Christian Monasticism*. Oxford: Oxford University Press.

Campbell, J. (1975). *The Hero with a Thousand Faces*. London: Abacus.

Cayley, D. (1992). *Ivan Illich in Conversation*. Concord, Ontario: Anansi.

Cocker, M. (2007). *Crow Country: A Meditation on Birds, Landscape and Nature*. London: Jonathan Cape.

Cornish, S. (2011). Negative capability and social work: insights from Keats, Bion and business. *Journal of Social Work Practice, 25*: 135–148.

du Plessix Gray, F. (1970). *Divine Disobedience: Profiles in Catholic Radicalism*. New York: Alfred A. Knopf.

Eliot, T. S. (1935). *Four Quartets: Burnt Norton*. In: *Collected Poems 1909–1962*. London: Faber and Faber, 1963.

Emanuel, R. (2001). A-void—an exploration of defences against sensing nothingness. *International Journal of Psychoanalysis, 82*: 1069–1084.

Emerson, R. W. (1992). Friendship. In: T. Tanner (Ed.), *Essays and Poems* (pp. 94–107). London: J. M. Dent.

Ficino, M. (1975). *The Letters of Marsilio Ficino, Vol. 1*. Members of the Language Department of the School of Economic Science, London (Trans). London: Shepheard-Walwyn.

Fink, B. (1996). *The Lacanian Subject*. Princeton, NJ: Princeton University Press.

Foucault, M. (2001). *Fearless Speech*. Los Angeles, CA: Semiotext(e).

France, P. (1997). *Hermits: The Insights of Solitude*. London: Pimlico.

Freud, S. (1912e). Recommendations to physicians practising psycho-analysis. *Standard Edition, XII*: 111–120.

Gilmore, T. (1999). Productive pairs: Briefing note. Philadelphia, PA: Center for Applied Research.

Goethe, J. W. von (1949). *Faust, Part 1*. P. Wayne (Trans.). Harmondsworth, Middlesex: Penguin.

Goldman, E. (1917). Love among the free. In: I. L. Horowitz (Ed.), *The Anarchists* (pp. 268–283). New York: Dell, 1964.

Grotstein, J. S. (2004). The seventh servant: The implications of a truth drive in Bion's theory of "O". *International Journal of Psychoanalysis, 85*: 1081–1101.

Grotstein, J. S. (2007). *A Beam of Intense Darkness: Wilfred Bion's Legacy to Psychoanalysis*. London: Karnac.

Hadot, P. (1995). *Philosophy as a Way of Life: Spiritual Exercises from Socrates to Foucault*. Oxford: Blackwell.

Heifetz, R. A. (1994). *Leadership Without Easy Answers*. Cambridge, Mass: The Bellknap Press of Harvard University Press.

Hinshelwood, R. D. (2008). Systems, Culture and Experience: Understanding the Divide between the Individual and the Organization. *Organizational and Social Dynamics, 8*: 63–77.

Keats, J. (1970). *The Letters of John Keats: A Selection*. R. Gittings (Ed.). Oxford: Oxford University Press.

Kirkpatrick, B. (Ed.) (1987). *Roget's Thesaurus of English Words and Phrases* (new edn). Harlow, Essex: Longman.

Kitto, H. D. F. (1957). *The Greeks* (reprint with revisions). Harmondsworth: Penguin.

Lacan, J. (1979). *The Four Fundamental Concepts of Psycho-Analysis*. Harmondsworth: Penguin.

Levine, D. (2001). The fantasy of inevitability in organizations. *Human Relations, 54*: 1251–1265.

Miller, E. (1998). Are basic assumptions instinctive? In: P. B. Talamo, F. Borgogno, & S. A. Merciai (Eds.) *Bion's Legacy to Groups* (pp. 39–51). London: Karnac, 1998.

Milner, M. (1987). *The Suppressed Madness of Sane Men: Forty-Four Years of Exploring Psychoanalysis*. London: Tavistock [reprinted London: Routledge, 1988].

Mitcham, C. (2002). The challenges of this collection. In: L. Hoinacki, & C. Mitcham (Eds.), *The Challenges of Ivan Illich: A Collective Reflection* (pp. 9–32). Albany, NY: State University of New York.

Needleman, J. (1990). *Lost Christianity: A Journey of Rediscovery to the Centre of Christian Experience*. Shaftesbury, Dorset: Element Books.

Newton, M. (2002). *Savage Girls and Wild Boys: A History of Feral Children*. London: Faber and Faber.

Nouwen, H. (1981). *The Way of the Heart: The Spirituality of the Desert Fathers and Mothers*. New York: HarperCollins.

Paulsell, S. (2005). Attentiveness. In: P. Sheldrake (Ed.), *The New Dictionary of Christian Spirituality* (pp. 135–136). London: SCM Press.

Peacock, J. Acceptance speech at "BBC Sport's Personality of the Year Awards", BBC 2, 16 December 2012.

Pieper, J. (1981). Die Verteidigung der Freiheit (The Defence of Freedom). In: J. Pieper *Lesebuch* (*The Josef Pieper Reader*), pp. 143–146. München, Kösel-Verlag.

Pieper, J. (1990). *Only the Lover Sings: Art and Contemplation*. L. Krauth (Trans.). San Francisco: Ignatius Press.

Prakash, M. S. (2002). A letter on studying with Master Illich. In: L. Hoinacki, & C. Mitcham (Eds.), *The Challenges of Ivan Illich: A Collective Reflection* (pp. 141–152). Albany, NY: State University of New York.

Snell, R. (2013). *Uncertainties, Mysteries, Doubts: Romanticism and the Analytic Attitude*. Hove, East Sussex: Routledge.

Spencer, E., & Pahl, R. (2006). *Rethinking Friendship: Hidden Solidarities Today*. Princeton, N.J. and Oxford: Princeton University Press.

Stafford, F. (2013). Preface to *Lyrical Ballads*. In: *William Wordsworth and Samuel Taylor Coleridge: Lyrical Ballads 1798 and 1802*. Oxford: Oxford University Press.

Steiner, J. (1985). Turning a blind eye: The cover-up for Oedipus. *International Review of Psycho-Analysis*, 12: 161–172.

Stephenson, R. H. (1995). *Goethe's Conception of Knowledge and Science*. Edinburgh: Edinburgh University Press.

Tracy, D. (1981). *The Analogical Imagination*. New York: Crossroad.

Vaill, P. (1998). *Spirited Leading and Learning*. San Francisco: Jossey-Bass.

Vanstone, W. H. (1982). *The Stature of Waiting*. London: Darton, Longman and Todd.

Weil, S. (1951). *Waiting on God*. London: Routledge and Kegan Paul [reprinted London: Fount, 1977].

Weil, S. (1986). *Simone Weil: An Anthology*. S. Miles (Ed.). New York: Weidenfeld & Nicholson.

Williams, R. (2014). What the body knows. *Resurgence and Ecologist*, 283: 34–35.

BIBLIOGRAPHY

In addition to the publications cited in the text and referenced above, we would like to offer some suggestions for further reading for anyone who wishes to explore further the way Bion's ideas on groups have been analysed and developed. The following list includes a comprehensive bibliography of works published up to 2008, general books on Bion and his life, and works that concentrate on group relations and on the application of his ideas, for example in organisational consultancy.

Banet, A. G., & Hayden, C. (1977). A Tavistock primer. In: J. E. Jones, & J. W. Pfeiffer (Eds.), *The 1977 Annual Handbook for Group Facilitators* (pp. 155–167). La Jolla, CA: University Associates.

Bion Talamo, P., Borgogno, F., & Merciai, S. A. (Eds.) (2000). *W. R. Bion: Between Past and Future. Selected Contributions from the International Centennial Conference on the Work of W. R. Bion, Turin, July 1997*. London: Karnac.

Bléandonu, G. (1994). *Wilfred Bion: His Life and Works 1897–1979*. C. Pajaczkowska (Trans.). London: Free Association Books.

Bott Spillius, E., Milton, J., Garvey, P., Couve, C., & Steiner, D. (2011). *A New Dictionary of Kleinian Thought, based on A Dictionary of Kleinian Thought, by R. D. Hinshelwood*. London: Routledge.

Brunner, L. D., Nutkevitch, A., & Sher, M. (Eds.) (2006). *Group Relations Conferences: Reviewing and Exploring Theory, Design, Role-Taking and Application*. London: Karnac.

Colman, A. D., & Bexton, W. H. (Eds.) (1975). *Group Relations Reader 1*. Washington, DC: A. K. Rice Institute.

Colman, A. D., & Geller, M. H. (Eds.) (1985). *Group Relations Reader 2*. Washington, DC: A. K. Rice Institute.

Cytrynbaum, S., & Noumair, D. A. (Eds.) (2004). *Group Dynamics, Organizational Irrationality, and Social Complexity: Group Relations Reader 3*. Jupiter, FL: A.K. Rice Institute.

Fraher, A. L. (2004). *A History of Group Study and Psychodynamic Organizations*. London: Free Association.

French, R., & Vince, R. (Eds.) (1999). *Group Relations, Management and Organization*. Oxford: Oxford University Press.

Gould, L. J., Stapley, L. F., & Stein, M. (Eds.) (2001). *The Systems Psychodynamics of Organizations: Integrating the Group Relations Approach, Psychoanalytic, and Open Systems Perspectives*. London: Karnac.

Gould, L. J., Stapley, L. F., & Stein, M. (Eds.) (2004). *Experiential Learning in Organizations: Applications of the Tavistock Group Relations Approach*. London: Karnac.

Grinberg, L., Sor, D., & Tabak de Bianchedi, E. (1993). *New Introduction to the Work of Bion, Revised Edition*. Northvale, NJ: Jason Aronson.

Grotstein, J. S. (Ed.) (1981). *Do I Dare Disturb the Universe? A Memorial to W. R. Bion*. London: Maresfield [reprinted with corrections London: Karnac, 1983].

Hinshelwood, R. D. (1987). *What Happens in Groups: Psychoanalysis, the Individual and the Community*. London: Free Association Books.

Hopper, E. (2003). *Traumatic Experience in the Unconscious Life of Groups. The Fourth Basic Assumption: Incohesion: Aggregation/Massification or (ba) I: A/M*. London: Jessica Kingsley.

Huffington, C., Armstrong, D., Halton, W., Hoyle, L., & Pooley, J. (Eds.) (2004). *Working Below the Surface: The Emotional Life of Contemporary Organizations*. London: Karnac.

Human Relations (1999). Special issue: Integrating psychodynamic and organizational theory. *Human Relations, 52(6)*: 683–852.

Karnac, H. (2008). *Bion's Legacy: Bibliography of Primary and Secondary Sources of the Life, Work and Ideas of Wilfred Ruprecht Bion*. London: Karnac.

Kreeger, L. (1975). *The Large Group: Dynamics and Therapy*. London: Karnac.

Lawrence, W. G. (Ed.) (1979). *Exploring Individual and Organizational Boundaries: A Tavistock Open Systems Approach* (pp. 169–192). Chichester: John Wiley (reprinted London: Karnac, 1999].

Lawrence, W. G. (2000). *Tongued with Fire: Groups in Experience*. London: Karnac.

Lawrence, W. G., Bain, A., & Gould, L. (1996). The fifth basic assumption. *Free Associations*, 6: 28–55.

Lipgar, R., & Pines, M. (Eds.) (2003). *Building on Bion: Branches—Contemporary Developments and Applications of Bion's Contributions to Theory and Practice*. London: Jessica Kingsley.

Lipgar, R., & Pines, M. (Eds.) (2003). *Building on Bion: Roots—Origins and Context of Bion's Contributions to Theory and Practice*. London: Jessica Kingsley.

López-Corvo, R. E. (2003). *The Dictionary of the Work of W. R. Bion*. London: Karnac.

Menzies Lyth, I. (1988). *Containing Anxiety in Institutions: Selected Essays, Vol. I*. London: Free Association Books.

Menzies Lyth, I. (1989). *The Dynamics of the Social: Selected Essays, Vol. II*. London: Free Association Books.

Obholzer, A., & Zagier Roberts, V. (Eds.) (1994). *The Unconscious at Work: Individual and Organizational Stress in the Human Services*. London: Routledge.

Palmer, B. (2002). The Tavistock paradigm: Inside, outside and beyond. In: R. D. Hinshelwood & M. Chiesa (Eds.), *Organisations, Anxieties and Defences: Towards a Psychoanalytic Social Psychology* (pp. 158–182). London: Whurr.

Pines, M. (Ed.) (1985). *Bion and Group Psychotherapy*. London: Routledge & Kegan Paul.

Sher, M. (2013). *The Dynamics of Change: Tavistock Approaches to Improving Social Systems*. London: Karnac.

Symington, J., & Symington, N. (1996). *The Clinical Thinking of Wilfred Bion*. London: Routledge.

Torres, N., & Hinshelwood, R. D. (Eds.) (2013). *Bion's Sources: The Shaping of his Paradigms*, (5–19). Hove, East Sussex: Routledge.

Trist, E., & Murray, H. (Eds.) (1990). *The Social Engagement of Social Science, Volume 1: The Socio-psychological Perspective. A Tavistock Anthology*. London: Free Association Books.

Turquet, P. (1975). Threats to identity in the large group. In: L. Kreeger (Ed.), *The Large Group: Dynamics and Therapy* (pp. 87–144). London: Maresfield [reprinted London: Karnac].

INDEX

hyperactivity and 27
impact on individuals 22, 32
inevitability of 37
interaction and 104, 114
losing the ability to think 137
Nouwen on 28
pain and 28
pairing and 110–111
potential for destructive
    impact 37
powerful hold of 32
purpose and 34–38, 119
purpose of 38
swift shifts to 36
turning away from the truth 71
unconscious motivation
    fuelling 27
vicious cycles 71
du Plessix Gray, Francine 73
dysfunctional behaviour xvi

Eliot, T. S. 40
emails 107
Emanuel, Ricky 12, 27, 47
Emerson, Ralph Waldo 109–110
emotion
    Armstrong on 28, 48
    attention and 21
    Bion and groups 1, 51–52
    case studies 4, 49, 84
    causing distraction 2–3, 51,
        86, 131
    containment of 13
    development arising from 70
    drives of obscure origin 31
    evenly suspended attention
        and 17
    groupishness and 60–62, 78, 89
    intelligence and 28
    pain and 29
    truth at the heart of growth 50
etymologies 10–11, 29–30, 52, 114

evasion 29
evenly suspended attention *see also*
        attention; focused attention
    complexity and 19
    contemplation and xv
    emotionally difficult situations,
        in 17
    focused attention and 1–2, 12,
        14–15, 27, 39, 59
    Freud on 12, 14
    fundamental importance of 12
    groups and their individuals
        32–33
    purpose and pursuit of truth
        12–13
    Roget's Thesaurus and 11
    sticking with awkward realities
        and 9
experience
    experiential learning 126–127, 138
    focusing on 125
    groupishness and 57
    groups, of 67–68
    immersion in 138
    making immediate judgments
        on 135
    previous experience 15
    unknown dimensions of 1
Experiences in Groups (Wilfred Bion)
        see also Bion, Wilfred; groups
    Armstrong and Bion on 141
    attention and 10
    common purpose 80
    cooperation 22
    dynamic of distraction 32
    dysfunctional behaviour
        examined xvi
    groupishness 55, 70
    invitations to test out ideas 140
    purpose of 36
experiential learning 126–127, 138
explanation, escape into 8

truth and 48
words giving impression of 46
knowledge 12, 48, 51

Lacan, Jacques 51, 137
language 46, 61, 71–72
leadership
    authority figures and 134–135
    common purpose and 80
    dependency of followers 96,
        112–113
    Masters degree module 116–117
    models of 123
    ordinary group members
        showing 136
    vision and 124
    withdrawal and 59
    yearning for 132
Levine, David 75
listening 113

malnutrition 50
Marks and Spencer 97
meditation 12
meetings xiv–xv, 90
Merton, Thomas 68
Mexico 73
military terminology, use of
    Bion's experience 80
    Boadicea analogy 123
    case studies 75–76, 106
    easily used 124
    fighting talk 106
    group animals at war 55–56, 73,
        89, 121
    sabotage of the group 78
Miller, Eric 70
Milner, Marion 2
Mitcham, Carl 72
Moses 111
motivation
    avoidance of pain 28

care and attention and 15
    fuelling distraction 27
    resisting responsibility 111
    vigorous individuality 89
motor racing 62
multilingualism 71–72 *see also*
        language
mythology 76, 111

narcissism 70
Needleman, Josef 8
negative capability xvii, 13–14
Newton, Michael 61
Nouwen, Henri 28

obedience 114
observation 14

Pahl, Ray 109
pain 28–29, 60
pairing 97–98, 109–112
    case studies 103, 136
    interpretations of 123
parrhesia 73
patterns of behaviour 95 *see also*
        interaction
Paulsell, Stephanie 10
Peacock, Jonnie 62
perception 2
personality clashes 53
perspective 60
Pieper, Joseph xv, 40, 50
polis 68
post traumatic stress disorder xvi
Prakash, Madhu Suri 73
prayer 15
"Pre-View" (*Experiences in Groups*) 22
previous experience 15 *see also*
        experience
productive pairs 110 *see also* pairing
purpose 79–93
    attention and 32–33, 45